PRAISE FOR
CONSCIOUS LOVE

"In *Conscious Love*, Christian de la Huerta charts the map of the heart like an architect designs a sacred space—with reverence, clarity, and an understanding that every crack, every shadow, belongs. This book reminds us that love is a landscape we must learn to walk with both courage and grace, where each step is a prayer, each relationship a mirror, and every moment an invitation to build the home we carry within ourselves. It is a powerful offering for anyone ready to reimagine the way we relate, connect, and belong in this world."

—**Richard Blanco**
Presidential Inaugural Poet
Author of *How to Love a Country*

"Having known Christian for over 30 years, I've watched his journey unfold with unwavering integrity, depth, and heart. In *Conscious Love*, he brings a lifetime of insight, spiritual wisdom, and hard-earned experience to one of the most essential topics of our time. This book is a powerful guide for anyone seeking relationships that are soulful, authentic, and truly transformative. I couldn't recommend it more."

—**Chip Conley**
NY Times bestselling author
Founder of the Modern Elder Academy

"Christian de la Huerta masterfully bridges the worlds of personal growth and intimate connection. *Conscious Love* is a powerful guide to emotional intimacy, personal transformation, and conscious relationships that reflect who we truly are. A must-read for anyone ready to love—and live—more consciously."

—**Lisa Haisha**
TV host, Author of *SoulBlazing*

"Christian de la Huerta's newest book, *Conscious Love: Transforming Our Relationship to Relationships*, is a profound exploration of what it truly means to connect with others from a place of authentic presence and love. This remarkable work illuminates the subtle dimensions of relationship dynamics that are often overlooked yet crucial for genuine connection. As someone who teaches conscious relationships in my Joy School, I am delighted to incorporate this wisdom into my curriculum, as it perfectly complements Joy School's core message that we already ARE the love we seek. Christian guides readers through a transformative journey that deepens our capacity to relate to others with intention, vulnerability, and heart-centered awareness—essential skills for anyone seeking to create relationships that generate growth, healing, and lasting joy."

— **Lisa McCourt**
Founder of Joy School
Millions-selling author of *Free Your Joy*

"In a world where so many are yearning for deeper connection and true intimacy, *Conscious Love* is a timely and profound offering. Christian de la Huerta brings the rare combination of spiritual depth, psychological insight, and lived experience to illuminate a path toward healing and wholehearted relationships. This book is a gift—one that invites us to show up with courage, presence, and authenticity in all our connections."

—**Jamie Catto**
Author of *Insanely Gifted*

"Christian de la Huerta changed my life years ago when he introduced me to breathwork. What I touched in that space—truth, laughter, empowerment—I'll never forget. In *Conscious Love*, he brings that same depth to the mess and beauty of relationships. This isn't some fluffy self-help guide. It's real. It's sharp. It's for people who are done living a mediocre life and ready to show up with clarity, guts, and soul. Christian doesn't sell the fantasy that love just happens. He shows you how to rise into it—with your eyes open. This book is a raw call to stop sleepwalking through your relationships. It unpacks all the ways we sabotage love—through ego, projection, codependence, and all the myths we cling to out of fear. Christian doesn't sugarcoat it. He hands you the mirror and asks you to do the work. But he also shows what's possible when two people choose to grow together, not just cling to comfort. Christian breaks it down step by step. Starting with how unconscious conditioning wrecks intimacy, and moving through personal healing, emotional responsibility, sexual awakening, and what it means to actually embody love—not just talk about it. It doesn't shy away from anything: power struggles, emotional immaturity, sexuality, spiritual hypocrisy—it's all here.

Bottom line: this isn't a love-and-light relationship manual. It's a guide for people ready to stop blaming, start owning, and actually show up—for themselves, and for love that's real."

—**Eli Nash**
Host of the *In Search of More Podcast*

"Christian de la Huerta has been focused upon mastery in the realm of relationships for decades. To that end, he's run popular retreats on conscious love. This book is a joyous celebration of every bit of wisdom he's learned on the way to that mastery. It demonstrates how to do love in the best way possible. It is comprehensive--a true roadmap to becoming the best giver of love, and the best receiver of love you can be. And the section on Sacred Sexuality is Divine!"

—**Dr. Susan Corso**
Author of *The Entergy Integrity Workbooks*

"By creating a roadmap from challenge to solution, Christian de la Huerta offers readers a clear direction to traverse the quest for conscious love. This book is a testament to the power of the hero's journey to see beyond their broken hearts and disillusionments and into their purpose of a boundless love with self and others. Another superb offering from one of the masters of the craft."

—**Roger Kuhn, PhD**
Author of *Somacultural Liberation*

"*Conscious Love* is a timely and necessary guide for a world in relational crisis. With clarity and compassion, Christian de la Huerta invites us to shift from unconscious patterns to intentional, empowered partnerships. This book isn't just about romance—it's a roadmap to reclaiming your power, healing deep wounds, and choosing love as a conscious path of growth and evolution. Insightful, practical, and deeply human."

—**Dr. Carol Talbot**
Leading the Evolution of Multi-Dimensional Intelligence
Author of *Re-Imagine You*
Keynote Speaker on Conscious Leadership & DNA Potential

"With clarity, compassion, and soul, Christian invites us to explore the deepest truths of our hearts. *Conscious Love* goes beyond romance—it's a call to courage, self-awareness, and the kind of emotional healing that sets us free to love ourselves and our partners more fully and fearlessly."

—**Terri Tate, RN, MS**
Author of *A Crooked Smile*

"Christian's new book, *Conscious Love: Transforming Our Relationships to Relationships*, struck me in a particular way on a number of fronts. First, the depth, an extraordinary grasp of the largest and smallest and all things in between—perspectives on this subject that concerns all of us. And then second, that the gestalt of what he is teaching and speaking of is actually about our relationship with life itself—with life and all that this brings to us in hopes, dreams, wishes, tasks and purpose. A school of learning this is—profound and real, caring and loving. These pages show us how to live our purpose for life, here and now."

—**Ed Schreiber**
Founder, Zerka Foundation

"Christian de la Huerta takes a deep dive into looking at relationships from angles people tend to miss. You can't read this and not think differently about your own relationships...and, perhaps, the greatest gift, is look at yourself in relationships with more kindness than you've ever allowed."

—Fay Thompson
Author of *So Help Me God* and *Azez Medicine*

"Christian de la Huerta provides the kind of guidebook I wish I'd had in my early twenties. *Conscious Love* is a soulful, gentle invitation back into alignment with ourselves—so that we might relate to others from a place of wholeness. This book offers a much-needed roadmap for anyone seeking healthier, more sacred partnerships of any kind. Christian reminds us that relationships aren't just about give and take; they are spiritual processes of awakening. Through each other, we grow, heal, and remember how to live with greater depth and expansiveness. With deep compassion and luminous insight, he shows us how to bring more magic, integrity, and meaning to the ways we love."

—Kaelan Strouse
Author of *Journey to the Ecstatic Self, I Dreamt of Flight,* and *48 Gateways to the Ecstatic Self*

"*Conscious Love* blends spiritual wisdom, psychological insight, and practical tools to help readers break free from fear-based limitations and step into their most authentic selves as they connect with others. Christian de la Huerta invites us to live powerfully, purposefully, truthfully, and with secure attachment in all our relationships."

—Jeff Lutes, LPC
Psychotherapist, Author of *Trailblazers in Love,* and Executive Director of The Center for Contemporary Relationships

"This book is pure relationship alchemy. *Conscious Love* should be required reading for anyone who desires to grow through the path of a fulfilling relationship. This book isn't just a guide to partnership, it's a mirror, a map, and a wake-up call. I highly recommend it!"

—**Tama Kieves**
TEDx speaker and bestselling author of *Learning to Trust Yourself: Breaking Through the Blocks that Hold You Back*

"Christian de la Huerta has struck gold once again. His masterful writing speaks directly to the heart, offering profound insights and timeless wisdom that only he can deliver. This book is a must-read if you're ready to be inspired and truly understand the art of conscious love. It has the power to elevate not only your relationship but your entire life."

—**Jaime Bronstein, LCSW**
"The #1 Relationship Coach Transforming Lives,"
by Yahoo Finance; Author of
*MAN*ifesting*; Host of *"Love Talk Live"* Podcast

CONSCIOUS LOVE

Transforming Our Relationship to Relationships

Christian de la Huerta

CONSCIOUS LOVE:
TRANSFORMING OUR RELATIONSHIP TO RELATIONSHIPS

© 2025 by Christian de la Huerta
All rights reserved.

Printed in the United States of America
Published by Soulful Hero Media
3191 Grand Avenue, #331763
Miami, FL 33133

All rights reserved. This book contains material protected under International and Federal Copyright Laws and Treaties. Any unauthorized reprint or use of this material is prohibited. No part of this book may be reproduced or transmitted in any form or by any means, electronic or mechanical, including photocopying, recording, or by any information storage and retrieval system, without express written permission from the author.

Library of Congress Control Number: 9781735059099
ISBN: 978-1-7350590-9-9 (Hardback)
ISBN: 978-1-7350590-7-5 (Paperback)
ISBN: 978-1-7350590-8-2 (E-book)
Available in paperback, hardback, and e-book

Book design by Publishing Services
Cover design by Aamer Ullah Khan
Cover Art by Lora_ecology
Illustration by Oscar Piludi
Author Photo by Peggy Callahan

Contents

Author's Preface xiii

Part I: The Call To Conscious Love

1. Introduction. 21
2. Unconscious Vs. Conscious Relationships 25
3. The Case For Conscious Relationships 31
4. The Top 10 Relationships Challenges 35

Part II: Top 10 Solutions To Relationship Challenges

5. The Expectation Trap 39
6. The Foundation For Conscious Relationships. 43
7. What Level Do You Choose? 47
8. More Than A Feeling 51
9. Ego Or Hero?. 55
10. Past Pain To Present Love 67
11. Our Relationships Require Maintenance 75
12. Help Wanted: Relationship Champions 85
13. Emotions Are Not The Enemy! 91
14. The Heart Of Connection 115

PART III: UNMASKING THE BARRIERS TO LOVE

15. What Are Your Obstacles To Love?............129
16. What Truly Drives Us?............................133
17. Beliefs That Break Relationships.............139
18. The Paradox Of Relationships..................145

PART IV: PAVING THE WAY FOR LOVE

19. Clearing The Space..................................153
20. Reclaiming Our Power In Relationships....159
21. Change: The Only Constant.....................167
22. Staying In The Cauldron.........................173
23. Navigating The Love Frenzy....................179
24. Clearing The Path To Love......................183

PART V: SACRED UNION: MERGING SEXUALITY AND SPIRITUALITY

25. Harmonizing Sexuality And Spirituality....189
26. Sacred Sexuality ... An Oxymoron?..........191
27. Ready To Bring Spirit Into Sex?...............195
28. So You Want To Be A Better Lover?.........197
29. Sexual Energy, Spiritual Power................203
30. Redefining Sexy: Beyond The Surface......207
31. Becoming Magnetic................................215
32. New Horizons In Sexuality.....................217
33. Outrageous Morality..............................219
34. Stages Of Morality: Evolving Beyond Right And Wrong..223
35. Sexual Ethics: (So ... Who And What Can We Do?)....227
36. Rethinking Celibacy And Monogamy.......231

Part VI: Embodying Conscious Love

37. Successful Relationships 239
38. Choose Love. 243
39. Embodying Conscious Love In Everyday Life. 247

Endnotes 249
About The Author 251
Index 253

AUTHOR'S PREFACE
The Heroic Act of Loving Consciously

For as long as I can remember, I've been fascinated by the mysteries of love—not just the romantic kind, but the deeper, quieter force that calls us to wholeness, challenges our fears, and awakens our souls. Love is, after all, the most powerful energy in the universe. And yet, it remains one of the most misunderstood.

Over three decades of personal transformation work, breathwork, and spiritual inquiry, I've witnessed how our relationships—whether intimate, familial, or communal—become the arenas where we either lose ourselves or remember who we are. They reveal the places where we're still hiding, still afraid, still clinging to old stories about our worth and our power. And yet, within those same relationships, we're given daily opportunities to wake up, to heal, and to reclaim ourselves.

Conscious Love was born from that space. It's a response to the loneliness, disillusionment, and disconnection so many of us feel in a world overflowing with hyper-connection but starving for depth. This book isn't about finding *the one*—it's about *becoming the one*. It's about realizing that love isn't something we stumble into, but something we consciously practice, nurture, and choose within ourselves and with others.

In a world that often confuses love with possession, control, or dependence, choosing to love consciously—with presence, courage, and authenticity—is a quiet rebellion. It asks us to dismantle inherited myths, risk vulnerability, and hold ourselves accountable for the ways we show up, both for others and for ourselves. In doing so, we reclaim the kind of love that heals, empowers, and liberates—a love that's far more than a fleeting emotion. It becomes a heroic act.

I once witnessed a woman in a breathwork session sob as she finally let go of the belief that she was unworthy of love. For years, she had carried that story like an invisible weight—woven from childhood wounds, cultural expectations, and heartbreaks that left her convinced she wasn't enough. In the safety of that sacred space, guided only by the rhythm of her own breath, something cracked open.

What began as trembling turned to tears, and those tears became the sound of an old identity unraveling. Breath by breath, she released layers of shame, doubt, and inherited myths about what love should look like, and who deserves to receive it.

I've witnessed moments like this time and again—people shedding lifetimes of fear in a single, honest breath. It reminds me how tightly we grip these stories: that love must be earned, that it requires sacrifice, or demands we shrink, perform, or pretend. And each time, I'm struck by how fiercely the heart longs to be free. To belong. To be seen without masks or defenses. To love without conditions.

That longing is why this book exists. *Conscious Love* is the next step in my Calling All Heroes series—born from the conviction that heroism today isn't about slaying dragons or conquering empires, but about facing ourselves. It's about healing the wounds that have shaped us, choosing truth over illusion, and loving with an open, undefended heart.

Why now? Because in a world so divided and weary of performance, what we need most is presence, authenticity, and soul-centered relationships. Ones that don't endlessly repeat our old patterns but help us remember who we truly are. I believe we stand at a turning point, and the consciousness we bring to love—to our connections—will shape not only the quality of our lives but the world we're creating together.

And why me? Because this has been my path—not as an outsider, but as a fellow traveler. I have lived these questions. I've stumbled in my own relationships, wrestled with my wounds, and sat in the fire of transformation again and again. As a teacher, facilitator, and seeker, I've had the privilege of walking beside countless others through heartbreak, awakening, and liberation. What I've learned—through ancient wisdom, modern psychology, breathwork, and the unflinching honesty of the human heart—I now offer here.

This book is not a prescription. It's an invitation. A call to remember that the love you long for isn't something you find—it's something you claim, cultivate, and courageously live.

This matters to me because I've seen what happens when people awaken to this kind of love. Lives shift. Relationships heal. Families mend. And it matters now because our times demand it—a love that is conscious, intentional, and free from the old scripts that keep us small.

So, dear reader—this is your moment.

I invite you to step into your own heroic journey. To say yes to love—not the neat, tidy version we've been taught to seek, but the raw, unfiltered force that transforms. The kind of love that asks us to shed old stories, face our wounds, and reclaim our wholeness.

Whether you're beginning this path or standing at a crossroads, may this book be a companion—a gentle nudge, a fierce mirror, a quiet whisper that you are not alone, and that you were made for this.

Because choosing love—conscious, courageous, imperfect love—is itself a heroic act.

It's time to say yes.

No matter what.

With love and gratitude,

Christian de la Huerta

Conscious Love

Transforming Our Relationship to Relationships

PART I

THE CALL TO CONSCIOUS LOVE

Chapter 1
Introduction
The Hero's Love Journey

Few things can take us to the heights of ecstasy and the depths of despair as quickly and as frequently as relationships. Few things knock us off balance as easily and disconcertingly. Few things capture our focus and consume our attention as completely. No doubt that is why entire industries exist for the purpose of enhancing the possibilities of love, sex, and relationships.

Love and relationships can make us feel as though we are on top of the world or plummet us into deepest doubt, darkest despair, and ruthless self-questioning, all in the space of seconds. They can make us hurt so bad that emotional pain becomes physical. Actual studies have confirmed a real heart problem called "Broken Heart Syndrome" that stems from loss, grief, and damaged relationships. [1]

The more I interact with participants in retreats, workshops, and other settings, the more evidence I find for the premise that most of us give our power away in romantic relationships. I consistently witness otherwise successful and empowered people selling out their power, too often just for a few crumbs of acceptance, validation, or pseudo-love. Otherwise self-defined and strong-minded individuals, who are established professionally and even spiritually, can lose their sense of self when it comes to intimate relationships. They surrender their power to escape loneliness, mistaking dependency for love.

Yet, such explanations provide only a partial answer, for these people often experience love and acceptance in other areas of their lives. Why are they not relinquishing their power elsewhere?

What is it about love relationships of the romantic variety that unhinge us so, that make us lose our minds and our center? Is it hormonal? A trick of nature? These answers seem insufficient, because the madness persists after the initial falling-in-love period, even in cases where we come to understand that this person may not be—and, in fact, often know *isn't*—the best match for us. Clearly, this is not a rational process.

The mysteries of attraction and love have yet to be deciphered by our species. We seem to be in the grip of forces far beyond our control that ignore differences in age, gender, belief, class, education, ethnicity, or even sexual orientation. Recent research, for instance, delves into the roles of scent and hormonal influences in shaping sexual attraction.[2] When caught in the grip of love's energies, our ability to think clearly seems to vanish. It's as though we're enveloped in a cloud or bubble, entranced by a spell, or drifting through fleeting moments of irrationality—brief lapses in clarity that defy reason.

Why do we lose our sense of self in relationships? The word *ecstasy* comes from the Greek *ek* which means "out of" and *stasis*, which relates to "standing." In ecstatic states we thus stand outside ourselves—our small selves. We become one and experience a collapse of ego boundaries that gives us a taste of freedom. In the presence of our beloved, time stops. The past and future fall away at times, and we find ourselves in the eternal moment. Though it may be brief and elusive, we want more of that!

In the frenzy of love, our emotions are off and running. We get high, literally, on the ensuing rush of endorphins, the release of hormones into the system. We are blinded by love, or at least, lust. We do and say things that we may later regret. Feeling unbound from the normal and predictable flow of our lives, we can be blinded to the possible repercussions of our acts and may end up dishonoring our bodies, placing our health at risk—and perhaps our families, careers, and futures. Nothing else matters in those exquisitely dangerous moments when in the throes of love.

But our madness also has its plus side. In this context of sexual/romantic relationships, we often let ourselves be more open and vulnerable. We allow ourselves to be truly seen.

Navigating relationships with consciousness is no simple feat—it's the work of true heroes. When we embrace this path, our healing and transformation accelerate significantly. In turn, our relationships gain a real opportunity for lasting success.

Here's the problem: In this crucial aspect of life—deeply tied to our core identity, survival, and self-worth—we lack the clarity, context, and skills needed to create successful, fulfilling relationships. Our educational and religious systems have fallen short in providing this essential guidance. It's the very reason I studied psychology in college, hoping to understand what drives us as human beings, yet found few practical insights to truly navigate the complexities of relationships.

Please note: The teachings in this book apply to all relationships—family, friends, and colleagues alike. However, our primary focus will be on romantic and intimate connections.

So let's dive in. What are conscious relationships anyway?

CHAPTER 2
UNCONSCIOUS VS. CONSCIOUS RELATIONSHIPS

The difference between unconscious and conscious relationships has to do with the level of awareness, intention, and responsibility each person brings to the relationship. Unconscious relationships are often driven by social conditioning, unexamined beliefs, unseen needs, habits, and behavior patterns; too often they have roots in unhealed past wounds.

Conscious relationships, on the other hand, are grounded in self-awareness, open communication, and a commitment to growth. Here's a brief look at some of the differences:

CONDITIONING VS. AWARENESS

In unconscious relationships, people often fall into patterns and behaviors without questioning them. They may be influenced by past experiences, family dynamics, or unexamined societal expectations. As a result, these relationships can feel repetitive or "stuck" because they are driven by ingrained habits rather than intentional choices.

Sarah always ended up doing most of the household chores while her partner, Mike, spent his evenings relaxing. This pattern persisted for years, causing resentment to build in Sarah. When she finally brought it up, Mike was surprised—he had assumed this division of labor was fine because it mirrored what he'd seen growing up, where his mother managed the home while his father worked long hours. Similarly, Sarah had taken on the role without question, influenced by a family dynamic in which her mother often emphasized and took pride in being "the glue that holds everything together."

Neither Sarah nor Mike had consciously chosen this arrangement; it was a pattern rooted in unexamined expectations from their pasts—an unspoken assumption that 'this is just the way things are done.' As a result, their relationship felt stuck, with Sarah feeling undervalued and Mike feeling blindsided by her frustration.

In conscious relationships, both individuals strive to bring awareness to their thoughts, actions, and emotions. They are willing to do the work to understand their own behavior patterns and make an effort to understand their impact on each other. Rather than acting and reacting on autopilot, they strive to choose behaviors that support mutual growth and connection.

REACTIVITY VS. RESPONSIBILITY

People in unconscious relationships tend to react impulsively to situations or emotions. For example, if one partner feels triggered, they may lash out or withdraw without reflecting on why they feel that way or how it affects the other person. This can lead to endless cycles of blame, defensiveness, resentment, and regret.

In conscious relationships, both partners take responsibility for their own feelings and actions. When a difficult situation arises, they practice pausing, reflecting, communicating openly, and owning their emotions rather than automatically projecting them onto the other person. This creates a healthier dynamic where each person is accountable for their part in the relationship.

PROJECTION VS. SELF-AWARENESS

Unconscious relationships are often plagued by projections, where individuals unknowingly attribute their own fears, insecurities, or unspoken desires onto their partner. A striking example of this came from a couple I worked with years ago. Lucia frequently accused her partner, Alina, of being unfaithful, despite Alina's repeated denials. Their relationship eventually ended, and the truth surfaced: It was Alina who had been having an affair all along.

Conscious relationships are grounded in self-awareness. Both individuals take time to understand their own needs, triggers, and vulnerabilities rather than projecting them onto each other. They recognize that each person is responsible for their own happiness and work to fulfill their needs from within before seeking it from their partner.

CONTROL VS. ACCEPTANCE

People in unconscious relationships often try to control each other's behaviors, emotions, or choices to feel secure. This can lead to manipulation, jealousy, or trying to "fix" the other person. This type of control usually stems from a fear of losing the relationship or a lack of trust in oneself and, therefore, the other person.

Henrietta and Francis were together for decades. She loved planning their weekends and wanted everything to go perfectly, but her need for control often crossed the line. She insisted on choosing the restaurants where they ate, the movies they watched, and even what Francis should wear to certain events. At first, Francis was comfortable with not having to make such choices at home because he felt burdened by the obligation of providing for their expanding family. But over time, he began to feel stifled, as though his preferences didn't matter. He grew hesitant to voice his opinions, fearing conflict or disapproval, and their relationship began to feel one-sided. Later in life, he began to exhibit delayed adolescent rebelliousness—challenging expectations in small but deliberate ways, such as reacting with veiled sarcasm or passive-aggressive remarks.

Conscious relationships are based on acceptance rather than control. Both people accept each other's individuality and are supportive of each other's growth. They trust that each person is on their own journey and let go of the need to control outcomes, which fosters a sense of freedom and respect. Their own self-acceptance and self-confidence allows them to go with the flow, creating more openness and flexibility in the relationship.

Dependence vs. Interdependence

In unconscious relationships, partners may rely on each other to fulfill unmet needs or to feel whole. This dependency can create a sense of obligation and lead to a lack of boundaries, where each person loses their sense of self in the relationship. Alan's partners were usually younger and, inevitably, in transition, not able to maintain their share of the financial aspects of their relationship. He began to discover that dependency eventually breeds resentment, on both sides.

> Dependency eventually breeds resentment, on both sides.

Conscious relationships value interdependence, where each person is whole and self-sufficient but chooses to share their life with the other. They support each other's growth and well-being without becoming enmeshed or dependent. This creates a balanced, healthy connection where both people can thrive individually and together.

Avoidance vs. Open Communication

Difficult conversations are often avoided in unconscious relationships because they are, by definition, uncomfortable. Sweeping challenging stuff under the rug inevitably leads to unresolved issues, passive-aggressive behavior, or simply a lack of true intimacy. Plus it's not an effective strategy. That stuff doesn't go away; it only festers under the surface. Over time, avoiding honest communication creates separation and resentment.

Like countless others, Amélie grew up in a generation conditioned to suppress their emotions. She buried her feelings, desires, and preferences deep within, until the pressure became unbearable and she erupted in frustration or anger, creating conflict in her relationships.

In contrast, open and honest communication is an integral aspect of conscious relationships. Partners are willing to experience the momentary discomfort of difficult conversations in order to work through challenges and understand each other more deeply. They listen actively, speak their truth courageously and with as much kindness and clarity as possible, creating a safe space for vulnerability. This kind of communication builds trust and deepens intimacy over time.

ATTACHMENT TO OUTCOMES VS. PRESENCE

People in unconscious relationships are often focused on specific outcomes or future expectations, like marriage, children, and certain milestones such as buying a house or financial stability. When these expectations aren't met, it can lead to disappointment or resentment.

Consider the case of Jake and Tara. From the beginning of their relationship, Jake envisioned a future where they would marry, buy a house, and start a family by a specific age. Tara, on the other hand, valued flexibility and wanted to focus on personal growth and traveling before settling down. Jake's unwavering focus on his timeline led him to interpret Lara's hesitation as a lack of commitment. Over time, his unmet—and, for the most part, uncommunicated—expectations fostered resentment, causing tension and frequent arguments. Meanwhile, Tara started feeling pressured and misunderstood, which made her withdraw emotionally. Their relationship suffered because Jake's focus on future outcomes prevented them from truly appreciating and navigating the present together.

Conscious relationships emphasize being present with each other rather than focusing on specific outcomes. Both people appreciate the relationship for what it is in the moment and trust the process of growth, wherever it may lead. They have learned to flow with life rather than struggle against the current. This openness fosters a sense of freedom and allows the relationship to evolve naturally.

FEAR OF GROWTH VS. EMBRACING TRANSFORMATION

In unconscious relationships, there can be a fear of change, as growth might disrupt the familiar dynamic. This can lead to boredom and stagnation, where each person resists personal development for the sake of preserving the status quo.

Take Aisha and Jose, for example. Aisha had been contemplating going back to school to pursue her dream of becoming a therapist, a goal she had put on hold for years. When she shared her plans with Jose, he reacted with subtle resistance, questioning the cost, the time commitment, and how it might change their lifestyle. Though he wasn't even aware of it initially, Jose feared that Aisha's growth might shift the dynamic of their relationship, making him feel less needed or left behind. Unconsciously, he began discouraging her, not realizing that his fear of change was holding both of them back from evolving as individuals and as a couple.

Conscious relationships embrace growth and transformation as an essential part of the journey. Both people are committed to their own and each other's evolution, even when it means facing uncertainty or stepping out of comfort zones. They recognize that individual growth ultimately strengthens the relationship, even if it temporarily rocks the boat.

CHAPTER 3
THE CASE FOR CONSCIOUS RELATIONSHIPS

By now I bet you're convinced that conscious relationships are the way to go, but here's the challenge: We're not very good at them. And yet, approaching relationships consciously is crucial because they deeply influence our emotional well-being, success, fulfillment, and overall quality of life.

Sadly, most of us are not equipped with the skills or awareness needed to navigate relationships effectively. As we have already seen, we often repeat unhealthy patterns, act on unexamined beliefs, or allow unresolved wounds from the past to shape how we connect with others. These dynamics can lead to unnecessary conflict, resentment, or disconnection. By bringing intentionality and self-awareness to our relationships, we not only improve how we relate to others but also unlock greater fulfillment, harmony, and balance in every other area of our lives—work, health, and even our sense of purpose. Conscious relationships become a foundation for thriving, not just surviving.

Relationship success or lack thereof is a complicated thing. Factors such as age, education level, income, and whether the couple has children can all influence the likelihood of divorce. Additionally, societal attitudes and cultural norms play a major role in shaping divorce rates.

Yet, imperfect as they may be, the numbers are telling. The percentage of marriages that end up in divorce differs widely around the world, depending on the country and specific demographic factors. For instance, while India and Chile have significantly lower rates, often below 5%, Sweden and Belgium have some of the highest rates, around 60-70%.[3] In the United States, the divorce rate is commonly cited as being around 40-50% for first marriages. Approximately 60-67% of second marriages end in divorce, and roughly 73-74% of third marriages don't make it.[4]

Clearly, we humans need some help in this area!

HEALTHY RELATIONSHIPS LED TO LONGEVITY

Here's one of the best reasons to want a conscious relationship: The cost of the alternative—being alone or stuck in unfulfilling relationships—is steep. Studies show that loneliness and social isolation can increase the risk of premature death by up to 50%, comparable to the health risks of smoking 15 cigarettes a day![5] Investing in meaningful, conscious connections is not just enriching—it's essential for our well-being.

Data backs this up. For example:

- Widowed individuals face a 39% higher risk of mortality.

- Divorced or separated individuals have a 27% greater chance of early death compared to married ones.[6]

And then there's the Harvard Study of Adult Development—an 80-year longitudinal study—that found close, supportive relationships are the single biggest predictor of long-term happiness and health, more so than wealth, fame, or social class.[7] Besides longevity, specific health benefits include improved physical health and mental and emotional well-being.

CONSCIOUS LOVE

Deepening our relationships IQ

Expanding our understanding of conscious connection offers far more than emotional fulfillment or improved health. It opens the door to a more purposeful, enriched way of living—both personally and collectively.

The transformative power of conscious relationships extends beyond the body and:

- Fosters Deeper Connection and Authenticity—Conscious relationships encourage open communication, vulnerability, and authenticity. This helps build deeper, more meaningful connections where both partners feel seen, valued, and understood.

- Reduces Conflict and Promotes Healthy Communication—When we approach relationships with awareness, we develop tools to navigate disagreements constructively. This reduces unnecessary conflict and helps resolve issues more quickly, avoiding the cycle of blame and resentment.

- Encourages Personal Growth—As we will dive into more deeply later, conscious relationships serve as mirrors, reflecting our strengths and areas for growth, creating opportunities to grow emotionally, mentally, and spiritually.

- Builds Stronger, More Resilient Bonds—Conscious relationships are built on trust, respect, and shared values. This foundation creates resilience, enabling the relationship to weather challenges and evolve over time.

- Teaches Emotional Intelligence—By learning to navigate emotions in ourselves and others, we build emotional intelligence, which not only benefits romantic partnerships but also friendships, family dynamics, and professional relationships.

- Prevents Toxic Patterns—A conscious approach helps us recognize and break free from unhealthy patterns like codependency, avoidance, or excessive control. This leads to healthier and more fulfilling connections.

- Enhances Self-Awareness—Investing in conscious relationships helps us understand our needs, boundaries, and triggers. This self-awareness empowers us to show up authentically and build relationships aligned with our values.

- Creates Ripple Effects in Other Areas of Life—Skills learned in conscious relationships—such as active listening, empathy, and mindfulness—can transform not only partnerships but also friendships, family ties, and professional collaborations.

- Contributes to a Healthier Society—Healthy relationships model positive behaviors for others, especially children, creating ripple effects in families and communities. Conscious connections pave the way for more compassion, understanding, and harmony in the world.

Ultimately, conscious relationships enrich not just our private lives but our experience of being human. They offer us a foundation on which to build a life of meaning, joy, and purpose.

> "LOVE IS WHEN YOU MEET SOMEONE WHO TELLS YOU SOMETHING NEW ABOUT YOURSELF."
> —ANDREW BRETON

So what holds us back from experiencing them? In the next chapter, we'll explore the hidden forces—emotional, cultural, and psychological—that often sabotage our relationships before they've even begun.

CHAPTER 4
THE TOP 10 RELATIONSHIPS CHALLENGES

Given the many benefits and importance of conscious relationships, what's the problem? Why do we have such difficulty finding and maintaining relationships that work? Unrealistic expectations lead to sabotaged relationships:

1) We approach relationships *with unrealistic expectations*—mainly, that they will fulfill or make us happy. Similarly, we bring along a constellation of often-unconscious beliefs and attitudes that interfere with our dreams and block our desires.

2) Settling is no way to start: We *sell out* to relationships that are not a real match, suppressing ourselves in order to avoid conflict or maintain the illusion of acceptance, validation, and love.

3) We seek without knowing what: We lack a *greater context* for relationships as an integral aspect of and as catalysts for our personal growth and spiritual evolution.

4) We chase the magnificent illusion: We confuse *falling in love*—the temporary, emotional, hormone-infused high—with the act and art of loving, the sacred work

of relationship. Additionally, our culture of immediate gratification and the "grass is greener" syndrome contribute to our jumping in and out of relationships, often prematurely.

5) The "I" disrupts our "we:" We lack understanding of *the ego* and its mechanisms. As a result, we get stuck in in bruising battles and destructive relationship patterns of being right, projecting, blaming, attacking and defending, and feeling like victims.

6) Our past rules the present: We carry around old unhealed wounds and unresolved past traumas that rear their ugly heads time and again in our relationships.

7) Our calendars eclipse our hearts: We struggle through busy and over-scheduled lives that leave little room for nourishing our relationships.

8) We navigate love blindly: We have few role models and support systems for conscious relationships.

9) We struggle speaking the heart's language: We have little understanding of our emotions and few skills as to how to deal with them.

10) Love gets lost in translation: We have not been taught effective, graceful, and empowered communication.

Let us now look at each of these challenges and consider some practical solutions and ways of expanding our understanding.

PART II

TOP 10 SOLUTIONS TO RELATIONSHIP CHALLENGES

CHAPTER 5
THE EXPECTATION TRAP

CHALLENGE #1: We approach relationships with unrealistic expectations—mainly, that they will fulfill or make us happy—and with a constellation of unconscious beliefs and attitudes that interfere with our dreams and block our desires.

SOLUTION #1: Approach love and relationships with consciousness by cultivating self-awareness and taking responsibility for your own fulfillment. See relationships as spaces for growth and connection, not validation or rescue.

We often enter relationships with an unconscious expectation that our partner will somehow complete us, fill the void within, or provide us with the meaning and validation we crave. This illusion of external fulfillment sets the stage for potential disappointment and resentment. We inadvertently place an immense and unfair burden on our partner, expecting them to be responsible for our happiness and fulfillment.

Right from the onset we give our power away whenever we look outside ourselves for validation or meaning. There isn't a single person out there who can fulfill us or make us happy. It is not their job, and it is not fair to impose that responsibility on anyone.

True fulfillment originates from within. It stems from a deep sense of self-worth, a connection to our inner values, and a commitment to personal growth. No one but ourselves can fulfill us, and to lay the responsibility for our happiness at another's feet dooms the relationship right from the start.

Relationships as Mirrors, Not Solutions

While relationships can offer companionship, love, and support, they are not a panacea for our problems. In fact, they can sometimes amplify our existing issues, bringing hidden insecurities and unresolved conflicts to the surface. Instead of viewing relationships as the solution to our unhappiness, we should recognize them as mirrors reflecting aspects of ourselves, both positive and negative. Placed in the right context, not only can they help take care of some basic human needs but also can speed up our spiritual evolution.

> The key to a healthy and fulfilling relationship lies in maintaining a strong sense of self.

This means cultivating our own interests, pursuing our passions, and nurturing our individual growth. We must be able to stand on our own two feet, without needing constant validation or approval from our partner. This doesn't imply detachment or isolation; rather, it fosters a sense of interdependence where both individuals thrive within the relationship while maintaining their unique identities.

The challenge is how to maintain a sense of who we are without needing to have that validated by the relationship or any other. The only way a relationship can really work is when we are aware of the fact that no one can provide us with a sense of worth. Only we can do that.

Our commitment therefore is to our own growth—and the growth of the other—above the shape and form of the relationship.

CONSCIOUS LOVE

THE ULTIMATE FREEDOM

The soul's true desire is for freedom—the freedom to be ourselves, to express our authentic selves without fear of judgment or rejection. This freedom extends beyond the confines of any particular relationship. It requires us to ask ourselves a profound question: "For the sake of my own liberation, am I willing to spend the rest of my life alone if it means living authentically and honoring my true self?"

> "WE WASTE TIME LOOKING FOR THE PERFECT LOVER, INSTEAD OF CREATING THE PERFECT LOVE."
> —TOM ROBBINS

By embracing this perspective, we can cultivate relationships that are not based on dependency or codependency, but rather on mutual respect, support, and a shared commitment to personal and spiritual growth.

POWER PRACTICES

The Myths That Shape Our Relationships

Many of us enter relationships guided by unconscious beliefs—stories we've inherited from culture, family, and past experiences. Some of these myths promise happily-ever-after fairy tales, while others instill fear, scarcity, or unrealistic expectations. But how many of them actually serve us?

By making a list of the myths we've absorbed about love, commitment, and partnership, we bring them into the light. This practice allows us to question which beliefs are helping us build conscious, fulfilling relationships—and which ones are quietly sabotaging our growth. Only by recognizing these hidden assumptions can we begin to replace them with truths that empower us. You can draw on the examples below to compile your own list. How do these myths apply to you? Are there others that have shaped your experience of love and relationships?

Common Relationship Myths

Idealization & Fairy Tales:

- "Happily ever after" is guaranteed.
- Love is always easy.
- Relationships are a permanent blissful state.
- Romance never dies.
- All hurts can be healed through a relationship.
- Only one "right" person exists.
- Finding "the one" will make me whole.

External Validation & Societal Pressure:

- Years together equals relationship success.
- Family/children equals relationship success.
- Social approval (family/friends) signifies success.
- Love equals physical beauty and sexual attraction.

Misconceptions About Relationships Themselves:

- Two people constitute the only valid relationship.
- Successful relationships mean an absence of conflict.
- Devotion is automatic and easy.
- "All I need is you" is true.
- Relationships keep loneliness at bay.

Misconceptions Regarding Sexuality & Gender:

- Sex is always gratifying.
- Sexual identity is permanently established.
- Fulfillment is unattainable in gay relationships.
- Men are incapable of monogamy.
- Gay relationships are not families.

CHAPTER 6
SELF-LOVE: THE FOUNDATION FOR CONSCIOUS RELATIONSHIPS

CHALLENGE #2: We sell out to relationships that are not a real match, suppressing ourselves in order to avoid conflict or maintain the illusion of acceptance, validation, and love.
SOLUTION #2: Yep, no way around it . . . if you want love, you gotta love yourself!

What a high price we pay to not feel alone! Too often we sacrifice our authentic preferences and values in a desperate attempt to avoid loneliness.

True self-love demands that we raise our standards. We become less willing to settle for anything less than genuine, authentic love. The more we love ourselves, the less we are willing to settle for morsels of pseudo-love.

> THE PATH TO PERSONAL POWER—AND CONSCIOUS LOVE—IS PAVED WITH SELF-LOVE.

Yet, true connection begins within. When we cultivate a deep sense of self-worth, the fear of abandonment disappears. We no longer feel the need to compromise our values for fleeting moments of acceptance. Ultimately, when we feel our connection to ourselves, we never feel alone, and we cannot be abandoned.

It requires a journey inward, a process of self-discovery that demands courage and introspection. The way in is the way out, and it has three phases:

- **A. Self-Knowledge.** That's the first stop on the hero's journey to conscious love. In ancient times the directive "Know thyself" graced the entrance to temples and other public buildings. First, we have to dive deep within and know who we are.

- **B. Self-Acceptance.** The next stage is when we attain such a deep level of self-acceptance that we are actually OK being "alone." Such a level of self-acceptance indicates a deep sense of meaning and purpose in our lives and an established connection to something greater. At that point everything else is icing—a gift and a blessing, but not the reason for our sense of purpose or the source of our happiness.

- **C. Self-Love.** Most of us by now know that it is impossible to love another unless we first love ourselves, and we cannot do that until we first know ourselves.

> "I DON'T TRUST PEOPLE WHO DON'T LOVE THEMSELVES AND TELL ME, 'I LOVE YOU.' ... THERE IS AN AFRICAN SAYING WHICH IS: BE CAREFUL WHEN A NAKED PERSON OFFERS YOU A SHIRT."
> —MAYA ANGELOU

ON THE PATH TO SELF-LOVE

Before we take the first step on the path to self-love, we make a conscious choice to free ourselves, to examine our belief systems and undo our conditioning, to dig deep and unveil the hidden layers underneath the lies and misunderstandings we have taken on. No one can do this work for us. Only we can do that. Of course we can get help along the way, ideally, trustworthy sounding boards, clear mirrors that will challenge as well as support us unconditionally and hold us to our highest standards potential. Yet, we are making the choice to become radically accountable, personally assuming ultimate responsibility for our lives. The buck stops here! Granted, stuff happened in our pasts that should never happen to anyone. We can't do anything about that. But we sure can do something about how we show up now in response!

We are committing to question the beliefs, mores, and dogmas handed down by family, society, religion, culture—a demanding process, certainly not one for the faint of heart and nothing short of heroic. We are willing to be wrong, to make mistakes, to fall short of the mark. We commit to doing the work to understand what the ego is, see how it operates in ourselves, to pull back our projections.

In a real sense we are engaging in a "holy war" with our own selves. Book 1 explored this deeper meaning of *jihad*—the inner struggle with the lower tendencies of the ego.

- Overriding our own reactivity, the need to be right and to win. Resisting the desire to strike back when someone does something hurtful, or to defend and erect walls when we feel attacked.

- Overcoming our ego's laziness and resistance, when it is time to go the gym or sit down and write.

- Letting go of the need to control people and circumstances.

The outcome of this holy war is self-knowledge, self-acceptance, self-mastery, inner peace. Eventually we free up energy from all the power-sapping effects of the inner struggle. There are no more games to play, and we discover freedom of expression: *I am who I am wherever I am, no matter what. I am whole and complete within myself and I stand alone if need be.*

That concept often found in pop songs and culture about "you complete me"? Nah, not really. No one can complete me. Only I can complete myself. Knowing that, you and I may choose to spend time together to enjoy our relationship and use it for our continued and unfolding process of healing, growth and evolution.

These three steps prepare the way and set the stage for conscious relationships. With that in place, and now from a place of free choice, how do we want to be in relationship? At what level do we wish to play? How deeply do we want to dive into this aspect of human experience? Once we get real about our expectations and accept the fact that a relationship is not the guaranteed solution to our existential issues of identity, purpose and self-worth, the next step is choosing the type of relationship we want to have. Are we ready and willing to use relationships as a vehicle for growth?

> "THE PURPOSE OF A RELATIONSHIP IS NOT TO HAVE ANOTHER WHO MIGHT COMPLETE YOU, BUT TO HAVE ANOTHER WITH WHOM YOU MIGHT SHARE YOUR COMPLETENESS."
> —NEALE DONALD WALSCH

CHAPTER 7
WHAT LEVEL DO YOU CHOOSE?

CHALLENGE #3: We lack a context for relationships as an integral aspect of and as catalysts for our personal growth and spiritual evolution.

SOLUTION #3: Reframe relationships as catalysts for growth and evolution, not just fulfillment or security. By understanding the Three Levels of Conscious Relationships, we can approach relationships with increased awareness, allowing for healing, self-discovery, and mutual awakening.

THE THREE LEVELS OF CONSCIOUS RELATIONSHIPS

Internationally renowned spiritual teacher Ram Dass spoke about two ways we can approach relationships: consciously or unconsciously. As we've been discussing, unconscious relationships are, regrettably, the status quo on our planet. People come together to try and fill a perceived need or lack in themselves through another person—a doomed effort right from the get-go. If we choose to take on relationships consciously, meaning that we are well aware that there isn't anyone out there who is going to make us happy—and how unfair to even place that expectation on someone else—there are three levels involved.

At **Level 1,** having fulfilled our basic needs for sex, intimacy, companionship, and perhaps family, we may find ourselves asking: "What's next?" Is there a deeper, more meaningful way to view and cultivate our relationships—a way that supports our own spiritual growth and evolution?

We can now reclaim the time and energy previously invested in the pursuit of these needs and redirect them towards our own personal and spiritual transformation.

This level could be taken on unilaterally, without the involvement of the other person, for they may not want to engage in this way. Needless to say, this does not imply we are using the other person for selfish reasons. Though they may not be contextualizing the partnership in the same way, we honor their innate worth and respect their needs and desires all the same.

By **Level 3** both partners are fully realized and in touch with their innate sacredness, realization, and divine heritage. As such, they revel in a sacred dance of embodiment, mirroring that for each other. Most of us don't need to worry ourselves with this one quite yet, so let's instead focus on **Level 2.**

Ready to Level Up? Relationship as Yoga

In **Level 2** relationships both partners agree to intentionally use the relationship as a vehicle for growth and a path to realization, to yoga, or divine union. A Soulful Relationship exists among people when—in addition to the love, companionship, intimacy, partnership, and/or sexuality found within the relationship—they consciously use their relationship as a vehicle for profound personal and/or spiritual growth. This is the path that most participants of Soulful Relationships retreats and, I assume, most readers of this book, are up for and interested in.

On this path, both partners agree to do the work of owning their emotions, busting their own egoic tendencies, recognizing their projections—in short, to use the relationship as a laboratory for transformation. They realize that if we want to shine a light on our blind spots—those parts of ourselves we cannot see and that are in need of healing—the best way to do that is to get in relationship. We humans are brilliant at discovering those buttons in each other and pushing them in the heat of an upset!

Let's be clear: Level 2 relationships are not a path for the faint of heart! They take work and relentless self-monitoring. Yet, they are so worth it! Though a demanding and heroic path, they will significantly accelerate our process of transformation.

Sometimes I think that the Dalai Lama has it easy being celibate! I am reminded of that story about the swami who finally emerges after spending 20 years in a Himalayan cave. Word gets out and soon she is surrounded by villagers who excitedly begin to press around her: "Master, Master, what have you learned?" "My children," she responds contentedly, "I have conquered anger." "Awesome!," they say, (because by now that irritating and overused expression has made it to every corner of the world) "and what else have you learned?" A little befuddled by their lack of appreciation for such an achievement, and slightly overwhelmed by the growing group around her, she repeats, "I've...conquered anger!" "Yeah, yeah, but what else?" "I have conquered anger!!!," she explodes in frustration, pauses, turns around and starts walking back to the cave.

Or as Hafiz would describe it in his inimitable way in "A Barroom View of Love:"

> "Love is grabbing hold of the Great Lion's mane
> And wrestling and rolling deep into Existence
> While the Beloved gets rough
> And begins to maul you alive.
> True Love, my dear,
> Is putting an ironclad grip upon
> The soft, swollen balls
> Of a Divine Rogue Elephant
> And
> Not having the good fortune to Die!"[8]

Approaching our relationships in this manner not only elevates them and provides a larger context for them, but also serves as a catalyst for our own growth. It is difficult to evolve in a vacuum. After five years in an ashram—which had its own set of challenges and opportunities for transformation, no doubt!—I got into a relationship and suddenly began to see patterns of behavior emerge that I thought I was done with.

The friction, the push and pull of relating, provides infinite opportunities for our emotional buttons to be triggered and our past hurts and unhealed areas to be exposed. For most of us, it is in intimate, romantic relationships that we allow ourselves to be most vulnerable.

With all this talk about the work of relationships, what about love? In the next chapter, we'll explore the question: What does love have to do with it?

CHAPTER 8
MORE THAN A FEELING

CHALLENGE #4: We confuse "falling in love"—the temporary, emotional, hormone-infused high—with the act and art of loving, the sacred work of relationship.

SOLUTION #4: When we view love as a sacred act rather than a fleeting emotion, we build the foundation for relationships that are not only lasting but deeply fulfilling. Embracing love as a daily choice to nurture, understand, and grow together allows relationships to transcend the honeymoon phase and thrive over time.

WHERE DOES THE LOVE GO?

When in the throes of "falling in love," especially during the honeymoon period, ego boundaries collapse and we feel a sense of oneness with the other. It's as if we are seeing through rose-colored glasses and the other person can do no wrong. That is, until the honeymoon period ends after six or nine months, maybe longer if we're lucky ... and haven't moved in together yet.

As Scott Peck brilliantly describes in *The Road Less Traveled*, this phase of falling in love is precisely that—a phase. It is a trick of nature, I think, to ensure the survival of the species. The hormones take over and blind us to flaws, foibles, and imperfections. At some point, perhaps when the other squeezes the toothpaste or replaces the toilet paper in the "wrong" way, ego boundaries come up again and suddenly we are asking ourselves: "Where did the love go?"

Reality has set in.

Too often, at this point, we walk away in search yet again of that elusive feeling of being "in love." Additionally, our culture of immediate gratification and the "grass is greener" syndrome work against us, encouraging us to jump in and out of relationships, often prematurely.

Peck's description of "falling in love" provides a great service, helping us to understand the difference: Love is not a *feeling*, but an *act*. Love is when we stretch our boundaries, sublimate or override our desires, our preferences, for the sake of growth—the spiritual growth—of another. Love requires that I expand beyond my comfort zone to include another.

None of this is to lessen the emotional experience of being in love. Who wants to caution another when they are in love? There are few feelings that are as all-encompassing and delicious; little else brings such ecstatic excitement, such juicy joy. Even the anticipation of being with our beloved can be rapturous. By all means, when you are blessed with it, enjoy it, revel in it, relish it, stretch it out as long as you can.

While being in love is one of the most delightful and fulfilling human experiences, it can be, at times, one of the most painful as well. Romeo and Juliet, a stirring, romantic, and tragic story, captures that uncontrollable urge to metaphorically devour the other person. If you have not seen the Franco Zeffirelli movie, you're in for a treat: It's an exquisite production with eye candy galore.

> "I BELIEVE IN LOVE THE VERB, NOT THE NOUN."
> —GREG BEHRENDT

Yet one of the reasons Romeo and Juliet's love has been immortalized is that they never got past the honeymoon period. We never saw what their relationship was like when they were married with children and struggling to pay bills after they both got disowned by their families and were driven out of town.

CONSCIOUS LOVE

LOVE AFTER THE HONEYMOON

But don't despair. The feeling of love *can* certainly outlive the honeymoon. While the initial euphoria may naturally fade, it makes way for something deeper and more enduring. The more we get to know each other, and as we realize that both partners are committed to their own growth and that of the other, the giddiness of the honeymoon period is slowly replaced with more grounded feelings of appreciation and respect. Companionship deepens, intimacy expands, and ideally, reverence emerges—a profound recognition of the gift we are to each other, especially when we approach love with consciousness, intention, and an open heart.

As we'll explore in greater depth later, sexuality can be a powerful gateway to profound spiritual experiences. Lovemaking has the potential to take us to both deeply intimate and elevated states of connection. Passion is not limited to the early stages of love—it can flourish, both in and out of the bedroom, as we learn to surrender more fully to each other and embrace the art of giving ourselves completely. In fact, as trust deepens and consciousness expands, intimacy can become even more exhilarating, transformative, and deeply fulfilling.

To paraphrase Peck, it is at the point when the honeymoon ends that the real work of loving begins.

CHAPTER 9
EGO OR HERO?

CHALLENGE #5: A lack of understanding about the ego and its mechanisms results in bruising battles of the egos, as we get stuck in patterns of being right, projecting, blaming, attacking, defending, and feeling victimized.

SOLUTION #5: If you want your relationships to have a chance to work, no way around it—you have to understand the ego and its shenanigans.

The ego, in its unexamined and unhealed state, is the root cause of human conflict, both on personal and global scales. It is the reason for both divorce and war. In personal relationships, the ego drives a wedge between partners by prioritizing being right over being connected, fostering patterns of blame, defensiveness, and unmet expectations. Over time, these ego-driven dynamics erode trust and intimacy, creating an emotional battlefield often culminating in estrangement or divorce.

The ego's need for control, power, possessiveness, and validation fuels societal and geopolitical conflicts. It manifests as intolerance, nationalism, and the relentless pursuit of "winning" at the expense of collective well-being. This can fuel societal divisions and ultimately lead to conflict and even war.

Understanding the ego's role is pivotal for healing these rifts. By becoming aware of its mechanisms—its need to protect, defend, project, and be right—we can begin to dismantle the barriers it creates. Cultivating self-awareness, embracing humility, developing empathy, and a willingness to see beyond our individual perspective are essential steps toward resolving conflict, whether in our homes or on the global stage. Only through this conscious effort can we move from separation to unity, from discord to peace.

In our closest relationships, the ego's influence can be particularly insidious. When we lack awareness of its influence, we can find ourselves locked in cycles of conflict—bruising battles where being right takes precedence over being connected.

These ego-driven dynamics lead to projection, blame, and defensiveness, creating an emotional battlefield rather than a space for mutual understanding. By cultivating self-awareness, we learn to recognize these ego-driven patterns, understanding how it seeks to protect us while often creating unnecessary walls. This allows us to create spaces for genuine connection, empathy, and healing, fostering deeper and more fulfilling relationships.

Reeling in our projections

In Book 1, we explored the ego in depth—its cunning tactics, manipulations, and the many ways it sabotages our happiness. I encourage you to revisit that section, as it holds invaluable insights into relationship dynamics, which often devolve into a battle of egos locked in power struggles.

One key area to address is the concept of projection. When we enter into a conscious relationship, a significant aspect of our growth involves recognizing and addressing our own projections.

In this context, it's a pretty safe bet that when we judge or make something wrong in the other, that it is also in us somewhere. If it's there, it's here. And the stronger our emotional reaction to someone's behavior, the more likely it is that we are being triggered by our own unhealed wounds and projecting our own unacknowledged or unresolved issues onto them.

To be clear, this does not excuse or condone anyone's behavior. It simply acknowledges that our reactions are often a reflection of our own inner state. We must always prioritize our own safety and well-being and set healthy boundaries in any relationship that is detrimental to our growth.

TURNING THE MIRROR AROUND

Conscious relationships offer a unique opportunity for self-discovery. Our partner can reflect back to us the unconscious patterns and unhealed areas that we may be unaware of—the blind spots in the back of our heads that we could not see otherwise.

One of the ego's arsenal of weapons is the handheld mirror, which it uses to shine a spotlight on the perceived faults and shortcomings of others, declaring, "You did this!" or "You always do that!" But as we learned, the more their actions get to us, the clearer the sign that we also do that, even if the details are different. That is the nature of projection. Seeing someone else's faults, mistakes, and shortcomings is easy; anyone can point the finger to criticize and judge. The tough, courageous work involves having the presence and humility to turn that mirror around and ask the hard question: "How do I do that?" That is nothing less than heroic.

If we truly want to illuminate the hidden, unhealed aspects of ourselves, there's no better catalyst than a relationship. Relationships have a remarkable way of exposing and triggering our deepest vulnerabilities—we're experts at pushing each other's buttons! Instead of falling into the typical ego pattern of reacting or defending, the work of soulful relationships invites us to pause, reflect, and turn the mirror around: "Ah, there's that old need to be right surfacing again. How predictable, exhausting, and boring! What's this really about? What's going on beneath that? Am I feeling unheard or invalidated?"

Or, "I'm feeling really pissed off by this conversation and all I want to do is lash out at my partner. What's really going on with me?" This practice of self-awareness and curiosity gently erodes the ego's need to being right, transforming conflict into a powerful opportunity for growth, understanding, and deeper connection.

For example, there was a time in one of my relationships when I felt unappreciated and disrespected, as though my wishes and requests were neither heard nor honored. Knowing how this dynamic works, I spent several days looking at all my relationships, trying to see where in my life I was dishonoring others. My good friends Jo and Steve, who honor sacred relationships this way, happened to be in town and in conversation I asked: "Help me see this. I haven't been able to figure out how it is that I am doing that." We kept on talking and suddenly she goes: "What about in relationship to yourself?" Oops. Had not looked there! A little later Steve asks: "And what about in your relationship to the Divine?" Wasn't looking there either!

More recently, I had started dating someone who all of a sudden started to flake out—not showing up or returning calls when he said he would. I didn't get it at first; my focus was still on him, wondering what was going on, especially after I called him at work and found out he was no longer employed there. My mind began to wonder: What's going on? Is it drugs? Was he fired? But I didn't get it. I was focusing on him. A week later I was trying to set up a meeting with a literary agent in New York who is normally very responsive, and nothing—not a word for a week. This one got my attention. Now it was two people from two separate areas of my life; I was no longer able to deny the common denominator.

Given the nature of blindspots, first I had to get clear: "What are *they* doing?" That part was easier to see: they were not showing up, not keeping their word or their agreements. The hard part, of course, is turning the mirror around: "How am I doing *that*? Where am I not showing up or keeping my word? Where am I out of integrity, not doing what I said I would do?"

It took me two or three days to get to it, but after an informal inventory of my relationships, the answer finally dawned on me: it was in relationship to my writing! How many times had I said that I was going to finish a chapter by a certain date and allowed myself to get distracted by email, social media, incoming calls, or other more "pressing" matters? Damn it! Busted! The details were different, but the dynamic the same. I wasn't showing up for my writing. That's how subtle and insidious projection can be.

The funny thing is that within an hour of my having that insight, they both called. As soon as I'd gotten the lesson, no longer did I need to create drama in my life so that I could see what had previously been lurking in the shadow.

> "WHEN YOU STRUGGLE WITH YOUR PARTNER, YOU ARE STRUGGLING WITH YOURSELF. EVERY FAULT YOU SEE IN THEM TOUCHES A DENIED WEAKNESS IN YOURSELF."
> —DEEPAK CHOPRA

Psychologist Carl Jung believed that we attract people into and create situations in our life to help us see our blindspots, those areas within ourselves that are in need of healing.

Reflecting on my life, I can now see distinct patterns in my relationships. In my first three, a recurring theme emerged: being cheated on. At the time, I didn't have the awareness to recognize the deeper dynamics at play, so I remained stuck in feelings of betrayal and victimization. However, with the tools of self-reflection, projection, and turning the mirror around, I might have asked myself an important question back then: "Since I am the common denominator in all three relationships, how am I doing the betraying?"

The answer is clear: While I was out to myself, my siblings, and close friends, I was still withholding a crucial part of my identity from my parents. I was also only partially open at work, confiding in just a couple of colleagues. At the time, I justified this by telling myself it wasn't a big deal—that I didn't want my parents to hurt or that my private life wasn't anyone's business. But the truth was, I wasn't free. In subtle but significant ways, I was lying about and withholding a core aspect of who I was. By keeping secrets, I was cheating myself and my relationships.

Since I had already begun teaching others about authentic living and embracing our true selves, I realized I could no longer lead a divided life. I made the decision to come clean and fully come out to my parents. From that point forward, my life became integrated—I was no longer hiding parts of myself or adapting who I was based on the situation. By embracing my whole truth, I stopped cheating myself and my relationship with my parents. Interestingly, the pattern of being cheated on has disappeared entirely and has not resurfaced in any relationship since.

Other challenges emerged over time, as they often do on the journey of self-discovery and growth. Later, I noticed a new pattern: attracting partners who either pulled disappearing acts or failed to show up fully in the relationship. These experiences were painful in their own way, leaving me feeling unappreciated and unsupported.

As I reflected on this trend, I realized that these partners were, in many ways, mirrors—revealing aspects of myself that still needed healing. Their inability to be fully present called attention to the ways I may not have been fully present with myself. Was I consistently honoring my own needs, boundaries, and values? Was I showing up for myself in the same way I expected others to show up for me?

These days, I pride myself on being reliable—keeping my word, following through on commitments, and renegotiating agreements when circumstances change. However, the pattern of not showing up occasionally resurfaces, particularly in my relationship with myself. This shows up most clearly when I procrastinate on my writing.

I can justify this procrastination with reasons, such as my lingering ambivalence about being in the public eye and the vulnerability that comes with sharing my thoughts. Yet, I recognize that this behavior ultimately undermines my mission. It's a subtle form of self-sabotage, keeping me from fully stepping into my purpose and sharing the insights I've been called to offer.

Addressing this requires the same honesty, commitment, and compassion that I bring to my external relationships. By showing up consistently for myself—especially in the creative spaces that call for courage—I align more deeply with my mission and ensure that I'm not shortchanging the impact I'm here to make.

With greater awareness—and after enduring enough of life's tough lessons—this pattern is finally loosening its grip on me. The encouraging truth is that the more we commit to doing our inner work, healing old wounds and tending to our personal growth, the less we find ourselves attracting unhealthy dynamics in our relationships. In essence, as we cultivate self-awareness and nurture our inner gardens, we create less drama in our lives.

This transformation doesn't happen overnight, but each step forward brings us closer to relationships and experiences that reflect the wholeness we've worked so hard to achieve. The work we do within ripples outward, allowing us to engage with others from a place of clarity, authenticity, and peace.

THE GIFT OF RESPONSIBILITY

One of the most salient characteristics of the ego—and one that often sabotages relationships and personal growth—is its tendency to remain stuck in victim mode. The ego thrives on blame and justification, finding comfort in pointing fingers at external circumstances or other people rather than turning inward to examine our own role in the challenges we face. This pattern not only keeps us entrenched in disempowerment but also creates barriers to authentic connection and self-awareness.

When we identify as a victim, we relinquish our power to change the situation, effectively handing over control of our lives to external forces and, often, the perpetrators. While it may feel temporarily comforting to avoid accountability, this mindset limits our growth and perpetuates cycles of pain and dissatisfaction. Breaking free from the ego's victim mode requires heroic courage, humility, and a willingness to reframe our experiences. To be clear, this is not about blaming ourselves but about reclaiming our power to create meaningful change in our lives and relationships.

Assuming responsibility for all aspects of our life can feel overwhelming at first. Yet, embracing this mindset holds immense potential: We lose nothing by trying it on, and the benefits—such as freedom and the empowerment of shedding a victim mentality—are transformative. Let me share a personal experience, my "Boss from Hell" story, to illustrate this principle.

Years ago, I worked in community relations at a psychiatric and addictions hospital. My boss was lazy, self-absorbed, and manipulative—a two-faced prima donna who often took credit for others' work, gossiped, and turned coworkers against one another. Despite her incompetence, she retained her position thanks to her friendship with the hospital administrator.

Six months into the job, I was fired. Corporate pressure to fill beds trickled down to our department, and I became the scapegoat when numbers didn't meet expectations. For years, I blamed her and her colluding, overcompensating, Little Napoleon of an administrator for what I felt was an unfair dismissal, judging them harshly for their actions—especially since they let me go two weeks before Christmas.

A SHIFT IN PERSPECTIVE

Eventually, I began asking myself different questions: Why did I create or attract this situation into my life? How did the experience serve me?

With honesty, I realized I had never really wanted the job. From the start, I felt disconnected from the hospital's demoralized staff, mediocre reputation, and profit-driven culture. My intuition told me to walk away, but I stayed out of fear—fear of financial instability, fear of the unknown.

Looking back, I see how I contributed to my own discontent. I allowed myself to be influenced by a toxic workplace culture of gossip and negativity, which drained my motivation. In truth, I had lost passion for the industry altogether and wasn't performing at my best. I had become disillusioned with the corporate-driven, cut-throat practices of an industry that was reacting to increased pressure from insurance companies. Had I known then what I know now, had I been in my power and able to live deeply in trust, I would have not taken that job.

CONSCIOUS LOVE

THE UNEXPECTED GIFT

Yet, in hindsight, getting fired was a blessing. It forced me to confront the deeper truths about my life's direction and prompted a radical shift. That New Year's, as I approached 30, I took stock of my life and set an intention to discover my true purpose.

Six months later, I left my next interim job, sold most of my belongings, and set out on a spiritual journey—from Miami to Hawaii and eventually California. That job turned out to be my last in the corporate world. Since then, I've devoted my life to teaching, leading transformational workshops and retreats, consulting, writing, and guiding others on their paths of growth and self-discovery.

We could then say that at a subconscious, perhaps at a soul level, I orchestrated this event to free myself and step into my life's purpose. In this scenario, my "Boss from Hell" played her role perfectly in my personal awakening.

CHOOSING EMPOWERMENT

When we fully own our lives—our choices, circumstances, and even our challenges—we step into a profound sense of freedom and empowerment. Some may argue that we aren't always in control, that external forces shape our reality in ways we cannot influence. While there's truth to that, choosing to take responsibility for our experiences—whether by learning from them, shifting our mindset, or taking intentional action—puts the power back in our hands. Whether this perspective is absolute truth or simply a powerful reframe is beside the point—what matters is that it sets us free, allowing us to respond to life consciously rather than feeling like passive recipients of fate.

Often, our "adversaries," those people who most aggravate us, turn out to be our best teachers, pointing us toward areas in need of growth and healing. That said, if you find yourself in an unfulfilling job or disempowering relationship, it may be time to liberate yourself.

Reframing Challenges as Opportunities

By reframing life's challenges as opportunities for growth, we pop ourselves out of victim mode and embrace ultimate personal accountability—and with it, the freedom to create a life aligned with our deepest truth.

The more we cultivate self-awareness and address the areas within ourselves that need healing, the less we find the need to unconsciously project our unresolved issues onto others. As we heal and grow, we naturally stop attracting people who mirror our blind spots and instead begin to draw those who are further along on their own evolutionary path. These individuals become companions in the truest sense—joining us on the journey not out of dependency or need, but because of the joy and mutual growth that comes from walking the path together.

When we no longer rely on others to fill our voids or validate our worth, our relationships shift to a higher vibration. Sharing life with someone becomes less about completing ourselves and more about enhancing the experience of living. With such companions, our journey becomes not only more enriching but also filled with moments of joy, connection, and the shared pleasure of discovery. Having someone to walk beside us in this way can make life's unfolding both more meaningful and infinitely more fun.

The Power to Shape Our Relationships

In focusing on the ego's tendencies toward projection and victimization, we open the door to profound growth and transformation. These patterns, while deeply ingrained, are not immutable; they can be unraveled with awareness, courage, and a commitment to self-reflection. By owning our experiences instead of blaming others, we reclaim the power to shape our lives and relationships.

The shift from victimhood to personal accountability is not just empowering—it's liberating. It enables us to break free from cycles of blame and stagnation, inviting instead a life of authenticity, freedom, and connection. As we take responsibility for our inner healing, we no longer need to attract the same challenging dynamics that mirror our unhealed wounds. Instead, we invite people and experiences that resonate with our higher potential and support our evolution.

Ultimately, the ego's illusions of separation, blame, and victim consciousness dissolve in the light of our willingness to take ownership of our own hero's journey. When we move beyond victim mode, we embrace the truth that life happens through and for us, not to us, allowing us to live with greater clarity, purpose, freedom, and joy.

> REMEMBER: WHILE WE MAY NOT CONTROL EVERYTHING THAT HAPPENS TO US, WE CAN ALWAYS CHOOSE HOW WE SHOW UP IN RESPONSE.

POWER PRACTICE

We have been exploring how whenever we find ourselves upset and our emotions activated, perhaps we are feeling self-righteous or victimized and easily spot a problem or flaw in our partner, we can safely assume that the behavior is also present in us in some way.

Consider the previous example with my disappearing date and the literary agent. In that situation, the more relevant questions was: Where was I not being accountable, not showing up? In relationship to my writing. As long as I focused on them and made myself the wronged party who was being dishonored, I gained or learned nothing, except the right to throw myself a pity party and wave my Poor Me sign around.

In other words, our job is owning our shadow. Accepting that we have a stake in the problem—and the solution. To help you reverse these projections, I have adapted the following four-step process from the work of Carole Kammen, founder of The Pathways Institute Mystery School.

1) What is the full story? Give words to the judgment. Get it out of your system. Don't be all evolved, spiritual, and understanding about it. Instead, let it rip: "That good-for-nothing SOB did this or that." Then ask yourself: How did I feel? Wronged? Victimized? Unseen? Unappreciated? Not valued? Abused?

2) When else in your life have you been in a similar situation or experienced a similar pattern that evoked those same feelings?

3) When have you behaved in that way in relationship to others?

4) When have you behaved in that way in relationship to yourself?

By the time you answer question #4, you likely will see a familiar pattern, only now you have information and tools for doing things differently, i.e., creating the solution.

CHAPTER 10
PAST PAIN TO PRESENT LOVE

CHALLENGE #6: We carry unhealed wounds and unresolved past traumas that resurface, often unexpectedly, disrupting and damaging our relationships.

SOLUTION #6: To cultivate healthy, conscious relationships, we must first confront and heal the wounds of our past. By recognizing and resolving old wounds, we break free from unconscious patterns and create space for love to grow unburdened by past pain.

WANT A GOOD RELATIONSHIP? HEAL YOUR PAST!

In Book 1 we saw that our unhealed egos are walking around in a state of emotional woundedness, marred by battle scars from our pasts. When these old injuries, these buttons, get pushed, we react in the present to previously similar situations that were never resolved. Which is what makes our relationships so fascinating and complicated: Not only are we dealing with current-day conflicts—which would be challenging enough—but at the same time we are working out stuff from our pasts!

We also considered the power dynamics patterns we attract into our lives, such as the tendency to give away our power or develop conflicts with people in positions of authority—teachers, bosses, ministers. These patterns are particularly evident in intimate relationships. It is as if we get stuck in repetitive behavioral loops, until we get it right. The actors may be different but it's the same boring movie. The packaging may change but the content is disturbingly familiar. At some point we must pause and ask ourselves: "Wait a minute—who is the common denominator in all these arguments, relationships, and power conflicts?"

As we then launch into the hard work of turning the mirror around, we begin by saying to ourselves: "OK, here I am again in what feels like suspiciously familiar territory. I really want to get the lesson this time so that I don't have to recreate this situation ever again. How can I show up differently this time? What can I learn from this now so that I can be done with it?"

Chances are that as we examine these patterns and why we do the things, we'll find ourselves tracing them back to their origin—our parents. No surprise there! As a friend puts it: *Of course our family knows how to press our buttons—they're the ones who installed them!* Our subconscious wiring is such that we become susceptible to reliving earlier dynamics of looking for love, acceptance, belonging, or validation by trying to recreate what we received or failed to get from our parents. As another friend, yoga teacher and author Darren Main, writes:

> "IT'S IMPORTANT TO HEAL OUR RELATIONSHIP WITH OUR PARENTS SO THAT WE CAN STOP DATING THEM!"

Now that's an additional incentive for doing this work!

Consider the following stories. Arnie began to experience stress and anxiety as we approached the completion of our private work together. During a session I asked about previous feelings or experiences of being abandoned in his life, which he promptly denied. Circling back around a bit later, I asked specifically about the relationship with his mother, to which he said, "No, on the contrary, she was overprotective and engulfing." A few days later he called to tell me he had remembered being told that as a newborn he had to be placed in an incubator and was kept away from his mother for several days. Bingo! With this new insight, he was able to stop the pattern of leaving his girlfriends before they could leave him.

Luis had a pattern of bucking up against his slightly older partner, and competing with him for attention in both social and professional settings. When he realized that he was really competing with his successful and accomplished father, their relationship improved dramatically.

Laura and Hassan both became aware of lifelong rescuing patterns that mirrored earlier relationships with parents who were either physically or mentally challenged. Because their mother suffered from a long, incapacitating illness, Laura, the oldest child, has spent her life rescuing first her siblings and then friends and colleagues from all sorts of situations. Hassan has had a series of relationships with women who are emotionally unstable, just like his borderline personality mother. His last girlfriend was probably borderline herself, exhibiting erratic and emotionally abusive behavior. Subconsciously, both were seeking to prove their worth, but their efforts faltered due to an underlying belief—a misunderstanding—that their value in a relationship depended on the other person needing to be rescued.

> "FORGIVE THE PAST. IT IS OVER. LEARN FROM IT AND LET GO. PEOPLE ARE CONSTANTLY CHANGING AND GROWING. DO NOT CLING TO A LIMITED, DISCONNECTED, NEGATIVE IMAGE OF A PERSON IN THE PAST. SEE THAT PERSON NOW. YOUR RELATIONSHIP IS ALWAYS ALIVE AND CHANGING."
> —BRIAN WEISS

As this last example illustrates, oftentimes we will escalate the pattern until it becomes so dramatic that it is impossible to deny. We should also point out that in part, that desire to rescue others is an authentic desire to help, an innate expression of a generous spirit. The problem is when things get twisted psychologically and the behavior is driven out of a subconscious need for validation or approval, as a way to feel good about ourselves, or whatever other subconscious need is driving it. At this level it becomes self-negating and insatiable. No matter how much we do, it will never be enough. In all likelihood, it will become detrimental to our own well-being.

YES, IT IS POSSIBLE TO HEAL OUR PASTS!

We are much greater than our traumas and our conditioning. There are various ways to get beyond all that. Tools such as psychotherapy, breathwork, or spiritual coaching can certainly help. There are a variety of modalities and countless practitioners available. How to find the right one? Ask your friends for referrals; look around; do your research. And most of all, trust your heart; make sure you feel comfortable in their presence and that they inspire trust. Personally, I would seek someone with a flexible approach, an open psychospiritual perspective, and the ability to help establish clear, specific goals. Don't be afraid of asking for references or testimonials. In most cases, this does not need to be an interminable, open-ended process.

Sometimes, specific life experiences can facilitate the necessary connections and rewiring for deep healing to take place. Eduardo, for example, had a long-standing pattern of dating significantly older men. That pattern persisted until he met a partner who truly saw, accepted, and validated him—someone who honored and authentically loved him at the core of his being. This experience served as "healing by proxy," allowing Eduardo to address and resolve a deep issue with his father through the presence of this substitute figure. After our work together, Eduardo's current partner is his own age, reflecting the profound shifts that took place within him. (For the record, I am not making intergenerational relationships wrong here at all, or saying they are only due to unhealthy dynamics.)

We can also heal past relationships unilaterally, even when the other parties are not available for whatever reason. As my former teacher Maia Dhyan would often say, we heal the past by being authentic, by taking a stand for ourselves in the present when we were previously unable to do so. It is like lighting a stick of dynamite with a long fuse into the past.

Yet again, the mantra of going within bears repeating. It's unavoidable, really. Besides reading this book and following the suggested practices, another option to accelerate your healing process is attending a retreat. These are specially designed to help participants get clear about their own individual obstacles to love, to personal empowerment, to fulfilling their life purpose. And they always offer a healing practice that I have found to be the most effective in healing past trauma. I call it "Spiritual Drano."

Just Breathe!

Breathwork is a perfect healing tool for the 21st century. Why? Because it works so fast and so efficiently, yielding immediate results and healing at every level: physically, emotionally, mentally, and spiritually. It is thus a perfect match for our over-scheduled, over-stimulated culture of immediate gratification.

It brings about immediate and profound relaxation and relief from the stress of daily living, while providing a sense of clarity and perspective in these often-confusing times. One session alone can change your life; its effects are immediate and permanent. Repeated breathwork practice brings about gradual yet powerful changes in a person's relationship to the world and other people, in their overall mood and life perspective, and in their sense of connection to Source, by whatever name you choose to call it. As if that were not enough, this simple, affordable, and accessible technique can be indescribably ecstatic!

In terms of healing past trauma, in all my years of exposure to transformational and healing work, I still do not know of anything that is more effective, nor which has such swift and direct effects. I have witnessed breathwork clients declare that they received more from a single session than from five to ten years of therapy. This is not to say that breathwork is a substitute for that often-valuable and highly beneficial process. Actually, it is a great adjunct to therapy, and can serve as a powerful catalyst to that process. Therapists will often suggest breathwork to their clients whose treatment may be stagnating or in need of a boost. Breathwork is a great catalyst for any other form of transformational or healing work in which we might engage, allowing for a more alive, full-body integration that can accelerate healing and positive change.

Why is this important? Lately, as I look around at my own life and that of those around me, it seems as if the pressure to implement change, to step more fully into whatever roles we have come here to fulfill, has been jacked up. It seems like old patterns are being released, sometimes so fast that it can feel like "spiritual Drano": all our old stuff—our old habits of behavior and/or systems of belief—are being cleared and flushed out!

People everywhere are changing life situations—jobs, relationships, patterns of behavior that are no longer sustainable—and freeing themselves from their self-inflicted and self-limiting prisons.

It is particularly during times of dramatic change that breathwork can smooth out the rough edges and facilitate the process of transformation. It can expedite change and help resolve both internal and external conflicts. When we work something out internally, we can often avoid the need to live it out through external—and often unnecessary—drama in our lives. Breathwork is a powerful way to unclog ourselves and release, in a graceful way, old pain, grief, anger, or other unexpressed emotions—stuff we have been schlepping around for way too long. Our normal M.O. in these matters—suppressing, ignoring, or trying to numb out or avoid these feelings by indulging in too much alcohol, drugs, ice cream, sex, shopping, TV, or social media—is a very ineffective way to deal with them. Just like energy cannot be destroyed but merely changes its form, repressed emotions get stored in our bodily tissues and surface as psychosomatic symptoms and disease. Often, when they finally come out, the results can be damaging to the people around us. Breathwork offers an alternative and healthy form of release for all these repressed feelings, emotions and trauma. And its effects are permanent.

Breathwork—especially when done regularly and over a sustained period of time—increases our peace of mind and sense of centeredness, even assisting us to sleep better. We feel enlivened, energized, and with clearer purpose. Ultimately, it helps us to find peace, simplify our lives, and make our relationships healthier and more alive. And incidentally, all this tends to have an anti-aging effect!

One last thing: Multiple consecutive sessions empower and compound the effects. This is the reason why our weekend retreats offer back-to-back sessions. So, breathe and breathe regularly!

> "THE LESS BAGGAGE WE CARRY, THE MORE ATTRACTIVE TRAVELING COMPANIONS WE BECOME ON THE JOURNEY OF LIFE. JUST BREATHE!"

As with anything else, buyer beware. There are different types of breathwork and practitioners, and while I would generally say that I would much rather have someone breathing than not, there are some that I would not be able to recommend. When looking for a practitioner, again, trust your intuition.

CHAPTER 11
OUR RELATIONSHIPS REQUIRE MAINTENANCE

CHALLENGE #7: Our busy and over-scheduled lives leave little room for nourishing and maintaining our relationships.

SOLUTION #7: Just like anything valuable in life, relationships thrive with care and attention. By cultivating the art of maintaining our relationships, we ensure that love doesn't wither under the weight of daily responsibilities but instead deepens and grows over time.

THE ART OF RELATIONSHIPS MAINTENANCE

There is no question that relationships take work. For those of us for whom that is a consideration, it is a valid one. They require attention and can just as easily be a source of comfort and happiness as one of conflict and distress. What makes the difference? Elevating them to the place of conscious relationships, which makes the work, pain, and discomfort always worthwhile—grist for the mill of our own evolutionary process.

Taking care of self and our relationships, that is, cultivating our individual and co-op gardens, is not optional. Simply, they are part of the job requirements for anyone on a spiritual path, and should be for anyone on the planet.

It comes down to choice and commitment. There is no universal decree that we have to be in a relationship to be happy. But if we do choose to be in one, we know that unless we take care of it and nourish it, it will shrivel and die.

Once the choice is made, there will be times when self-discipline is required to follow through on this commitment. When faced with the temptation to crash in front of the TV and sweep unspoken issues under the proverbial rug, choose differently. Instead of avoiding, take the time to connect, to talk, to air what's lingering in the space. Make the hard choice; take the higher road.

By summoning the courage to bring these issues into the light and engage with them openly, we make possible the opportunity to harvest their deeper yield. This practice of addressing and resolving, rather than avoiding, is not only a high choice—it is a heroic one, fostering growth, clarity, and authentic connection.

And, though I don't have children myself, I have enough of them in my life to realize that they take the demands of relationship to a whole other level. When working parents come home to the responsibility of children vying for attention, needing feeding and help with homework ... I get it. And I empathize. But there's still no way around it. If you want a healthy relationship, you will have to find a way to nourish and maintain it.

How do we keep the spark alive?

Where does the love go? These are perennial questions in the history of love and relationships.

And now we know the answer: If by "love" we mean that elusive and illusory feeling of being in love, good luck! As exquisite and all-consuming as that feeling is—one for which kings have abdicated thrones, faces have launched a thousand ships, and countless lives have been sacrificed—it will always be fickle, impermanent, and unpredictable.

But if we are talking about keeping relationships juicy, alive, and passionate, then we have something to talk about. Relationships thrive not by chance, but through intention and effort. There are practical ways to keep them functional and enlivening, and to address challenges as they arise:

- Maintain clear and open communication. By nurturing our co-op garden with care, keeping the space for relating open and clear, we prevent the "weeds" that choke relationships—such as resentment, misunderstanding, and neglect—from taking hold.

- Commit to keep an open heart. Keep the love alive, no matter what. We honor and cherish love, no matter what. Even in moments of hurt or anger, resist the temptation to shut down or close your heart. Honor and cherish the love that exists between you, allowing it to serve as an anchor through difficult times.

- Breaking free through forgiveness. Keeping the heart open means forgiving no matter what, even when that feels impossible. Forgiveness is a gift we give ourselves, not just the other person. When we're holding someone over the fire for what they did or failed to do, our hand is also getting burnt. Letting go of grievances liberates us, creating space for healing and deeper connection.

- Heed the call to adventure. Cultivate a sense of adventure and embrace the element of surprise to keep your relationship fresh and exciting. Routine and predictability can quickly lead to boredom and dissatisfaction, dulling the spark that brought you together. Keep the magic alive by continuing to woo your partner—show them they're cherished and never take them for granted. A little spontaneity and thoughtful effort can go a long way in keeping the connection vibrant and alive. And it doesn't have to be grand gestures. Little things go a long way.

- Cultivate generosity. Generosity is a cornerstone of thriving relationships. It's not just about material gifts but about giving of yourself—your time, attention, affection, and understanding. Be generous with your compliments, your patience, and your willingness to truly listen. Celebrate your partner's successes as if they were your own, and offer kindness even in moments of tension or disagreement. And yes, sometimes this takes heroic effort! Generosity fosters a sense of safety and trust, reminding both partners that the relationship is a place of abundance, not scarcity. When we approach our connections with an open heart and a giving spirit, we create an environment where love can flourish and deepen over time.

- Dance with give and take. Learning the flow of giving and receiving is essential for balanced and fulfilling relationships. Too often in retreats, participants share that they are more comfortable giving and struggle with receiving, sometimes to the point of feeling guilty or unworthy when others offer love, support, or kindness. This imbalance often stems from deep-seated issues related to self-esteem and self-worth, where one's value is tied to what they can do for others rather than simply being worthy of care and attention.

  Receiving requires vulnerability—a willingness to open up, trust, and allow others to show up for us. It challenges the ego's belief that self-reliance is strength and that accepting help or love is a sign of weakness. Yet, when we allow ourselves to receive, we affirm our own worthiness and create space for deeper connection. Learning to embrace this flow can be transformative, as it not only heals our relationship with ourselves but also enriches the dynamic of giving and receiving in all our interactions.

In this way, we cultivate a sense of harmony, where both partners feel valued, supported, and seen.

- Keep things in greater context. Keeping a broader perspective is essential in relationships. Our connection with the Divine and our spiritual evolution must remain primary, taking precedence over the form or structure of any relationship. Relationships are not the ultimate goal but rather a vehicle for growth, a conduit through which both individuals can evolve. As such, the form of a relationship may need to shift or evolve over time to better serve that growth. The true aim is to cultivate a sense of freedom, wholeness, and completeness within ourselves, independent of whether we are in a relationship or not.

Tending Love's Fire

Have you ever witnessed the creation of fire? It is such a profound privilege, one that strikes a chord deep in our ancestral memory.

Fire, to our modern minds, is as simple as striking a match, flicking a lighter or—going back to elementary school science experiments—using the sun and a magnifying glass. The actual creation of fire, however, is a complex endeavor that requires much effort, preparation, and focus.

Similarly, though its initial spark might be as simple as lighting a match, maintaining a relationship is a complex endeavor requiring effort and attention. Using a bow, string, and spindle stick to make fire is not easy, and neither is keeping a relationship alive.

When building a fire, the first order of business is finding the right location. We need to be mindful, for example, of where the wind is coming from and which way the smoke will flow, yet aware that it could all change in an instant. In our own lives our relationships are impacted by external conditions and circumstances over which we have little control. Unpredictable winds of change such as the economy, employment status, illness, or accidents can throw us for a loop. The characteristics of our living space and physical environment can significantly influence both our feelings about and the dynamics of our relationships.

Next, the area where the fire will be built requires cleansing and preparation. Just as we create a circle of safety, containment, and protection around the fire, we must do the internal work of clearing obstacles to love within ourselves. This is part of "cultivating our garden"—removing the stones, branches, and debris that can hinder growth. By clearing these internal blocks, we create a space for love to flourish, enabling us to attract a compatible partner rather than subconsciously sabotaging the process. This internal preparation also helps minimize the potential for conflicts, allowing for a more harmonious and fulfilling connection.

Finding the right kind of wood is important. Some burns more easily than others; some burns too fast; some is smokier than others; some can even be toxic when burnt. In Spanish the word for wood, *madera*, can also be used in reference to having the right mettle, caliber, or character. What kind of qualities are you looking for in a partner? In yourself?

Another preparatory step is building a little nest to capture the initial spark out of twigs, dry grass, moss and other tinder material. If there is no container to catch the spark and hold it, where it can be tended to, it will not survive. The same can be said about relationships; the container here applies to physical, psychological, emotional, and spiritual space.

How the wood pile is structured is important. Allowing room to breathe is critical; if the wood is placed densely, the flame can be stifled. Within a pyramidal structure we add twigs at first, gently, then larger kindling. What is the foundation of your personal fire? Is it steady, balanced? Can it hold the weight and keep the flame of love going or will it come crashing down? Who is your support system? Leaning on our partners for our happiness and fulfillment is not only suffocating; it is unfair and a sure recipe for failure. We need to give each other time and space to breathe, and the responsibility for fulfilling our life's purpose is ultimately ours.

CONSCIOUS LOVE

Friction creates fire. Once we create and capture that initial spark of fire, we need to maintain it. To keep the flame going we blow ever so gently on it; it is more like breathing on it, breathing it to life. Love, too, usually requires a little friction. Too much alikeness can be stagnating. When we are blessed with the unpredictable spark of love, we must tend it carefully, lovingly, ever attentive to and mindful of its needs. During times of friction, breathe! Deep breathing has an immediate calming effect and helps navigate the emotional reactivity, bringing choice back into the equation.

Once the fire is going, we still need to mind it, as the weight of the logs shifts or the wind changes direction. We will need to make adjustments, reposition logs, adding new ones—new sources of energy and life. Add too much and we stifle it, too little and the fire can go out. Similarly, our relationships require constant vigilance and maintenance, but not oppressively or breathlessly. The important thing is to be present, conscious, mindful—paying attention and making necessary course adjustments. Flexibility is key, and the willingness to let go of the way things were for how they now are and what they may become.

Love is in the details. By gifting them with our attention we discover what our partners like, what turns them on, physically and spiritually. For that is how the heart is wooed, seduced. Surprising them with little gifts—even a flower, book, stone, or crystal—just to let them know we are thinking about them, lets them know we have made an effort to know who they are and what they like. When we email them a song or an article that we know will interest them, they know that we were paying attention to what they were saying and what ignites their passion. When we give them something, such as a framed photograph that captures a special moment, we promote its remembrance and ritualize the relationship.

This is how we become tenders of the fire of love: We listen to the whispers of their soul. We become soul whisperers.

Asking for what we need, and finding playful ways together to meet those needs, is equally important. For though we are fire keepers, in a relationship we are also deeply a part of the fire itself. Indeed, that is at the heart of the creation of fire...we become one with it. In the words of Teilhard de Chardin:

> "SOMEDAY, AFTER MASTERING THE WINDS, THE WAVES, THE TIDES AND GRAVITY, WE SHALL HARNESS FOR GOD THE ENERGIES OF LOVE, AND THEN, FOR A SECOND TIME IN THE HISTORY OF THE WORLD, MAN WILL HAVE DISCOVERED FIRE."

POWER PRACTICE

Like a creeping vine, boredom and routine can strangle the life out of a relationship, causing the initial spark to flicker or even die as predictability takes over. The following are practices for injecting novelty and new experiences, as a way to keep the spark alive. Why not try invest in your connection by committing to one each week for the coming month?

1. The "Adventure Jar" Practice:

- The Invitation: Grab a jar and some slips of paper together. This week, each of you will secretly write down three new and relatively easy-to-do activities you'd both be open to trying. These could be visiting a museum or art gallery, trying a new type of cuisine, exploring a local park you've never been to, or attending a free outdoor concert.

- The Commitment: Fold your slips and drop them in the jar. Each weekend for the next month, randomly pick one slip and commit to doing that activity together, no matter what. Embrace the spontaneity!

- The Reflection: After each adventure, take a few minutes to discuss what you enjoyed and what you learned about each other through the experience.

2. The "Growth Share":

- The Invitation: This week, each of you will identify one thing you'd like to learn more about or a small step you want to take towards personal growth. This could be reading an article, listening to a podcast, practicing a new skill, experiencing breathwork, or reflecting on a challenging emotion.

- The Commitment: At the end of the week, dedicate time to share what you learned or experienced with your partner. Be open and vulnerable about your growth journey.

- The Reflection: How did sharing your personal growth with your partner impact your connection? How can you continue to support each other's individual development?

3. The "Dream Dialogue":

- The Invitation: Set aside dedicated time this week for a "Dream Dialogue." This is a space to openly share your individual dreams, both big and small, without judgment or interruption.

- The Commitment: Each partner gets equal time to share their aspirations. The other partner's role is to listen actively, ask clarifying questions, and offer support and encouragement.

- The Reflection: What new understanding did you gain about your partner's inner world and desires? How can you actively support them in pursuing their dreams?

4. The "Active Together Ritual":

- The Invitation: Commit to being physically active together at least twice this week. This could be a walk or bike ride along the river or at a park, a swim in the ocean, trying a paddleboarding session, or even just stretching together in the morning.

- The Commitment: Schedule these "active together" times in your week and treat them as important appointments. Be present and enjoy the shared movement.

- The Reflection: How did moving your bodies together impact your energy levels and your connection? What did you appreciate about your partner during this shared activity?

CHAPTER 12
HELP WANTED: RELATIONSHIP CHAMPIONS

CHALLENGE #8: In today's world of fractured communities and constant digital distractions, we often lack visible role models and support systems for cultivating conscious relationships. Without clear guidance, many find themselves struggling to navigate and sustain meaningful connections.

SOLUTION #8: We need relationship champions who can hold space for each of the partners—and for the relationship itself.

Creating a Relationship Support System

Cultivating a relationship is no small task—we need all the support we can get. Yet, too often in times of conflict, others take sides, fueling our grievances and reinforcing disempowering feelings of victimization: "How could that bastard do that to you?" "I can't believe what that bitch said to you!"

Starting in the Middle Ages, a champion was the regent's advocate and representative, someone who had the king or queen's back and even substituted for them in battle when necessary. This tradition has faded out now, but why not resurrect it? We could all use a champion for our relationships. What a boon it would be to have someone both parties could go to, who would listen with understanding and compassion and call everyone to their highest good—a clear mirror that would reflect to each their role in the conflict and highlight opportunities for growth.

That is quite a tall order: to hold space for each of the partners—honoring their growth above and beyond the shape of the relationship—while at the same time holding space for the relationship itself.

Perhaps the only way to reconcile these potential conflicts of interest is by asking the question: What is the highest good?

This question shifts the focus from individual desires or temporary discomforts to a more expansive, long-term perspective. By considering what is best for both partners' growth as well as the relationship's well-being, we can find solutions that honor both. Sometimes this might mean making sacrifices or adjusting the dynamics of the relationship, but ultimately it allows both partners to evolve in ways that align with their greater purpose. When both individuals thrive, the relationship itself becomes a powerful source of transformation and support, making room for deeper connection, love, and shared growth.

Imagine a future where relationships are widely viewed through this lens of champions, with enough of us skilled and experienced to offer genuine, meaningful support to one another. Perhaps we could even create couples' buddy systems or relationship support circles—communities of mutual care and guidance—to help navigate the journey together. In the meantime, that role can be filled by professional counselors or coaches. Perhaps we need a new job title: relationship champions!

IT TAKES A VILLAGE

Another improvement I hope to witness is our developing a sense of community in regard to relationships. When I officiate at a wedding or union ceremony, for example, I include and evoke the participation and investment of those present, so that the couple feels their support. I say something along the lines of: "We, those who know and love you, have a vested interest in your relationship. We want it to work out and commit to being there for you." While that is a beautiful and powerful ritual, I look forward to the day when those communities develop a way to provide support in a way that makes a difference.

Building robust relationships goes beyond the couple; it thrives within a supportive community, or "village." This network combats the isolation couples often feel, reminding them they are not alone in their challenges. Access to collective wisdom, shared experiences, and diverse perspectives empowers them to navigate difficulties with greater understanding and resilience. The normalization of relationship struggles reduces stigma and fosters emotional well-being, while practical assistance eases burdens during challenging times.

Furthermore, a village encourages accountability and personal growth, offering constructive feedback and modeling healthy relationship dynamics. Shared rituals and traditions strengthen bonds, while neutral third parties can provide invaluable perspective during conflicts. In times of adversity, the community acts as a stabilizing force, fostering unity and shared strength. Ultimately, a "village" promotes collective healing, addressing systemic issues that negatively impact relationships and cultivating a nurturing environment where love can flourish, strengthening both the couple and the wider community.

> "LOVE MAKES YOUR SOUL CRAWL OUT FROM ITS HIDING PLACE." —ZORA NEALE HURSTON

The external support of a community can bolster relationships, but it's the internal journey that truly determines their success. Building conscious relationships necessitates a deep dive into our own emotional landscape, a journey of self-discovery and empowerment. And that's we'll focus next, on the essential work of emotional mastery.

POWER PRACTICE

Relationship Support Circles

True transformation doesn't happen in isolation. As valuable as inner work is, healing and growth often flourish most powerfully in connection—with others who are also committed to living and loving more consciously.

This section offers a framework for Relationship Support Circles—intentional gatherings where couples come together in mutual support, accountability, and shared exploration. These circles are designed not to fix or judge, but to hold space, offer reflection, and build a sense of community for those navigating the journey of conscious love.

Whether you're looking to strengthen your bond, overcome persistent patterns, or simply share this path with others who understand its challenges and joys, this kind of relational community can become a profound source of insight and encouragement.

You don't need to be an expert to begin. All that's required is a willingness to be honest, present, and open-hearted—and a shared agreement that your relationship deserves to be nurtured not just privately, but in a larger container of care and collective growth.

Consider exploring these ideas with one or two other couples, or reaching out in our online community at Unleash Your Inner Hero (https://www.facebook.com/groups/unleashyourinnerhero), to find others who are also ready to take this next brave step together.

By fostering a sense of shared responsibility and mutual growth, these Relationship Support Circles can create a foundation of trust and encouragement, helping couples navigate challenges and deepen their connection.

Below are some suggested elements and activities to help structure your Relationship Support Circle:

1) Regular Check-Ins

- Monthly or Biweekly Meetings: Couples gather to share updates, challenges, and successes in their relationships.

- Guided Discussions: Facilitated by a trained coach or experienced couple to keep the conversation productive and focused.

2) Peer Mentorship

- Buddy Pairing: Each couple is paired with another for mutual support and accountability.

- Skill Sharing: More experienced couples share insights or strategies with those facing specific challenges.

3) Skill Building

- Communication Exercises: Practicing active listening, conflict resolution, or expressing needs.

- Role-Playing Scenarios: Rehearsing common relationship challenges in a safe, supportive setting.

- Resource Sharing: Exchanging books, podcasts, or tools that have been helpful for others.

4) Emotional Support

- Safe Spaces: Providing a judgment-free environment for couples to voice concerns or frustrations.

- Empathy Practice: Members listen without offering unsolicited advice, focusing on understanding and validation.

5) Goal-Setting and Accountability

- Shared Intentions: Couples set relationship goals and update the group on progress.

- Accountability Partners: Members gently hold each other accountable for commitments, such as scheduling date nights or attending therapy sessions.

6) Celebrating Milestones

- Acknowledging Successes: Celebrating anniversaries, breakthroughs, or resolved conflicts together.

- Rituals or Traditions: Creating shared activities, such as lighting a candle or offering affirmations for the group's collective growth.

7) Conflict Mediation

- Neutral Mediation: A trained facilitator helps couples work through disagreements during group sessions.

- Learning from Others: Observing how other couples handle similar issues can provide inspiration and solutions.

8) Community Building

- Social Events: Hosting informal gatherings to strengthen bonds outside structured meetings.

- Shared Activities: Participating in workshops, retreats, or service projects to build unity and shared purpose.

9) Crisis Support

- Emergency Contact System: Offering immediate support to couples experiencing significant struggles.

- Resource Network: Connecting members with therapists, counselors, or other professionals as needed.

CHAPTER 13
EMOTIONS ARE NOT THE ENEMY!

CHALLENGE #9: We have limited understanding of our emotions and even fewer skills to navigate them effectively.
SOLUTION #9: Mastering our emotions is the work of true heroes—an act of deep self-responsibility and inner strength. By cultivating emotional courage, discipline, and gracefulness, we shift from being ruled by our emotions to owning them fully.

ADRIFT IN THE EMOTIONAL SEA

Despite how deeply emotions shape our lives—our decisions, relationships, and sense of self—most of us have very little understanding of them. We experience emotions constantly, yet few of us have been taught how to recognize, process, or express them in healthy ways. Instead, we often suppress, ignore, or misunderstand our feelings, leaving us emotionally illiterate in a world that increasingly demands emotional fluency.

My father was a brilliant man and a highly respected psychiatrist—something I've heard time and again from those who worked with him. Yet, when it came to his own emotions, he was clueless. Likewise, I've seen countless psychologists, therapists, coaches, priests, and ministers who, despite their expertise, were also completely at a loss in terms of their own emotions. As Jesus is quoted as saying, "Physician, heal thyself!" (Luke 4:23). We must first tend to our own inner world if we are to truly support and guide others.

From a young age, we receive messages about which emotions are acceptable and which should be hidden. We learn to label certain feelings as "good" and others as "bad," leading to shame, avoidance, or overreaction when we experience them. Add to that the complete lack of emotional education in schools and workplaces, and it's no surprise that so many of us feel overwhelmed by our emotions or disconnected from them altogether.

Nowhere is this more evident than in our relationships. When we don't understand our emotions, we struggle to communicate them effectively, leading to misunderstandings, resentment, and conflict. Unprocessed feelings from the past spill into the present, shaping our reactions in ways we don't fully comprehend. We may find ourselves repeating unhealthy patterns, shutting down in moments that require openness, or expecting others to "fix" emotions we haven't learned to navigate ourselves. It's tragic: We don't even know why we do the things we do!

And worse yet, we also try to manage and control others' emotional experience! "Shh. Don't cry." "Stay strong." "Calm down!" "Keep a stiff upper lip." "Suck it up." "Stop being so sensitive." "You made your bed, now lie in it." "What doesn't kill you makes you stronger." Add to that the spiritual bypassing often seen in spiritual circles: "Love and light!" "It's all an illusion." "Everything is perfect as it is." "Choose love over fear." "Everything happens for a reason." "Just think positively." "You're just creating your own reality." "Just let it go." "Stay high vibe! / Don't lower your frequency." "It's all good."

While many of these perspectives hold elements of wisdom and truth from a higher vantage point, this pressure to always be "positive" can also dismiss essential emotions like anger and grief, oversimplify deep wounds that need genuine healing, and discourage necessary action toward change. At their worst, they risk invalidating someone's pain or struggles, even shifting blame onto the individual rather than acknowledging systemic challenges or real trauma.

Further complicating this is the "The Social Media Happiness Illusion." With the rise of curated online personas, there is pressure to present only the highlights of life, leading people to feel isolated in their struggles because they compare their real emotions to the seemingly "perfect" lives of others.

This chapter explores why we struggle with emotional awareness, how societal conditioning has shaped our disconnect, and what we can do to develop the skills necessary to navigate our emotional world with clarity and confidence. Becoming aware of our emotions is the first step toward emotional freedom—and it's never too late to learn. When we do, not only do we heal ourselves, but we also create deeper, more authentic, and more fulfilling relationships.

WHY ARE WE SO CLUELESS ABOUT OUR EMOTIONS?

The challenges we face with emotions stem from a combination of cultural, psychological, and personal factors. Here are some key reasons why those pesky emotions can be difficult to navigate:

1. *Cultural Conditioning*

Cultural conditioning leads to suppressing emotions and emotional illiteracy. In many cultures—particularly in the West—there is a strong emphasis on logic, control, and self-sufficiency, often at the expense of emotional awareness and expression. I believe that was the root of my father's denial of emotions. The all-powerful mind was meant to rule, and emotions were weakness. When people are implicitly taught to suppress or ignore their feelings, this leads to discomfort, awkwardness, and shame around emotional experiences. And we always have to pay the piper. My younger brother, Luis, drowned in a freak river boat accident in the Thames when he was 26. His death was devastating to our family, but I never saw my father cry. I'm sure he believed he had to "keep it together" for the sake of the family. Yet, a year later, to the day, my father was hospitalized for the first time in his life.

From an early age, we are conditioned by societal norms, family expectations, and cultural narratives that dictate how we should engage with our emotions. We are taught, directly or indirectly, that emotions are a sign of weakness, that vulnerability should be avoided, and that rationality reigns supreme.

The problem is that when emotions are repeatedly suppressed, they don't just disappear. They become buried, often manifesting in subtle ways—chronic stress, anxiety, physical ailments, or unhealthy coping mechanisms like addiction, overwork, or emotional numbness. The inability to recognize and process emotions creates a disconnect between our internal experience and our external behavior, leading to confusion, reactivity, and unresolved emotional baggage that affects our relationships, decision-making, and overall well-being.

2. Gender Norms

Traditional gender roles often dictate how emotions should be expressed. For example, men may be taught to suppress vulnerability, while women may face judgment for expressing anger or assertiveness.

From an early age males are taught that "boys don't cry" and told to "man up," reinforcing the idea that emotional expression—particularly sadness or fear—is unacceptable. The implication, of course, is that the emotions—and the feminine—represent weakness, both faulty assumptions. The emotions are not good or bad, strength or weakness; they are simply energies coursing through our bodies. Depending on how we express them they have a good or bad effect. And if you want to talk about strength, courage, or resilience, let's talk about the power of creation that resides in women's bodies!

Girls, on the other hand, may receive messages that their emotions are "too much" or "overly dramatic," often being dismissed, minimized, or mocked for expressing strong feelings.

Phrases like "You're too sensitive," "Stop overreacting," or "Don't be such a drama queen" subtly reinforce the idea that their natural emotional responses are excessive, irrational, or even burdensome to others. This not only teaches girls to distrust their own emotions but also conditions them to downplay their feelings in order to be accepted or taken seriously.

Over time, these ingrained beliefs create a deep-seated internal conflict. Many women grow up questioning whether their emotions are valid or whether they have the right to express them at all. This self-doubt can lead to emotional suppression, where they learn to bypass their feelings to avoid judgment or rejection. Instead of expressing anger, they might swallow it to appear "agreeable." Instead of asserting their needs, they may prioritize others' comfort over their own. This emotional restraint can manifest as chronic stress, anxiety, people-pleasing tendencies, or even difficulty setting boundaries in relationships.

3. Fear of Vulnerability or Loss of Control

Emotions are deeply personal and revealing. When we express them, we open ourselves up to the reactions of others—whether that be acceptance, understanding, judgment, or rejection. As we've established, many of us have been conditioned to believe that vulnerability is a weakness, making emotional openness feel risky or even dangerous. We can feel uncomfortably exposed. We may fear that if we let someone see our sadness, disappointment, or fear, they will think less of us, take advantage of our openness, or withdraw their support.

As a result, we learn to suppress, mask, or intellectualize our emotions rather than experience them fully. This fear of emotional exposure can manifest in behaviors like deflecting serious conversations with humor, avoiding deep connections, or retreating into silence when emotions become intense. Over time, this self-protective habit can create emotional distance in relationships, making it harder to truly connect with others in an authentic way.

Another important factor leading to emotional suppression is fear of losing control. Strong emotions—especially ones like anger, grief, or deep sadness—can feel overwhelming, unpredictable, and even threatening. Many people fear that if they allow themselves to fully experience these emotions, they might spiral out of control, saying or doing things they regret.

> "WHAT IS LOVE? THE TOTAL ABSENCE OF FEAR, SAID THE MASTER. WHAT IS IT WE FEAR? LOVE, SAID THE MASTER."
> —ANTHONY DE MELLO

True emotional strength comes not from avoidance but from developing the capacity to sit with our emotions, allowing them to move through us without becoming consumed by them. When we learn to embrace our vulnerability and regulate our emotions in a healthy way, we gain deeper self-awareness, emotional resilience, and more meaningful connections with others.

4. Lack of Emotional Education

Many people struggle with emotional awareness simply because they lack the language to describe what they're feeling. From an early age, emotional expression is often reduced to basic labels—happy, sad, angry—without deeper nuance. However, emotions are complex, and without a broad emotional vocabulary, it becomes difficult to process and express feelings in a healthy and meaningful way.

For example, someone might say they feel "stressed" when, in reality, they are experiencing a mix of frustration, disappointment, and overwhelm. Or they might say they feel "angry" when, in reality, they are experiencing a mix of hurt, fear, and a sense of betrayal. Without the ability to accurately name their emotions, they may struggle to address the root cause or communicate their needs effectively. Emotional literacy—the ability to recognize, name, and understand emotions—is a crucial skill that many people never formally learn. We'll circle back to this in a bit.

Buried Alive: The Costly Price of Bottling Up Emotions

While it may seem like pushing emotions aside helps maintain control or avoid discomfort in a relationship, emotional suppression comes with significant consequences—both mentally and physically. Ignoring or repressing emotions doesn't make them disappear; instead, they often manifest in unhealthy ways over time.

By now, we know we can't simply sweep emotions under the rug. Emotions are energy in motion. When we suppress them, they don't vanish; they get stored in the body. Over time, unprocessed emotions build up, leading to chronic stress, anxiety, depression, or even physical ailments such as tension, headaches, digestive issues, or high blood pressure. As the book *The Body Keeps the Score* illustrates, unresolved emotions don't just disappear—they linger beneath the surface and often resurface in unexpected ways.

Further complicating the problem, after years, decades, a lifetime of suppressing emotions, we accumulate layers upon layers of unresolved emotional baggage. When we try to build relationships in the present, everything gets filtered though all that unhealed trauma and buried feelings, distorting our perceptions and interactions. The result? We end up projecting our past wounds onto each other. Yikes! No wonder we struggle with relationships!

Plus, they have to come out one way or another. We suppress, suppress, suppress… and then Boom! Volcanic eruption. Bottled-up emotions can explode in moments of anger, sadness, or frustration, often disproportionately to the situation. These reactive outbursts can damage relationships, careers, and self-esteem, creating more harm than if the emotions had been addressed earlier.

Or we suppress, suppress, suppress… and the emotions start seeping out and showing up as physical symptoms: cancer, heart attacks, ulcers.

As we can see, suppressing emotions negatively impacts both personal well-being and relationships. It triggers the body's stress response, leading to increased anxiety and emotional exhaustion. This emotional distance harms relationships by hindering honest communication and fostering resentment. Furthermore, suppressed emotions often manifest as unhealthy coping mechanisms, like overeating or substance abuse, and inhibit personal growth by blocking access to vital self-awareness and learning opportunities. Essentially, avoiding emotions leads to a cascade of negative consequences, undermining both individual health and interpersonal connection.

MASTERING OUR EMOTIONS: THE STUFF OF HEROES

Mastering our emotions is an act of courage, self-responsibility, and inner strength—the work of true heroes. Rather than being ruled by our emotions, we can learn to own them fully, allowing them to inform rather than control us. This shift not only empowers us but also strengthens our relationships and fosters deeper connection, understanding, and trust.

By mastering our emotions, we also create space for others to do the same, breaking free from reactive cycles and co-dependent patterns.

The goal is to *have* our emotions, not to be *had* by them. Here's how to begin:

- Take full ownership of your emotional experience. No one can make you feel anything—your emotions are yours to process and understand.

- Let others have their emotional experience. Stop trying to manage or control how others feel. Mastering your own emotions is a full-time job—and one of the highest acts of personal empowerment.

- Build awareness. Becoming conscious of your emotions is the first step toward mastering them. Before reacting, take a breath, notice what you're feeling, and choose your response intentionally.

True emotional mastery is a journey, not a destination, but every step you take brings more freedom, clarity, and depth to your relationships.

THREE KEY COMPONENTS OF EMOTIONAL MASTERY

On the journey to emotional mastery, three essential pillars provide a strong foundation: emotional courage, emotional self-discipline, and emotional gracefulness. Together, they help us navigate our emotions with awareness and intention.

- **Emotional Courage.** Expressing our emotions requires vulnerability, and vulnerability takes courage. It means allowing ourselves to be seen, sharing our feelings honestly even when it feels uncomfortable, and embracing the risk of rejection or misunderstanding. True emotional courage is not about suppressing emotions but about showing up authentically, even in the face of fear.

- **Emotional Self-Discipline.** Mastering our emotions isn't about denying or repressing them; it's about having the awareness and discipline to *choose* how we express them. Rather than reacting impulsively or lashing out, emotional self-discipline allows us to pause, process, and communicate our feelings in a way that aligns with our values and intentions. This prevents unnecessary conflict and fosters deeper understanding.

- **Emotional Gracefulness.** How we express our emotions is just as important as the emotions themselves. Emotional gracefulness is the art of sharing our feelings in a way that others can truly hear, understand, and receive our communication. It's about finding the balance between honesty and compassion, between directness and kindness. When we speak with emotional gracefulness, we create space for connection, healing, and mutual understanding.

Developing emotional courage, discipline, and grace strengthens our emotional intelligence (EQ), fostering inner strength and agency in communication, conflict resolution, and resilience. This empowers us to elevate our relationships, creating space for deeper connection and mutual understanding. By taking ownership of our emotional experience, we break free from reactive cycles and build relationships grounded in authenticity and respect, affirming our personal empowerment.

Increasing Our E.Q.

So how do we cultivate emotional literacy?

The journey to emotional awareness involves learning to recognize, understand, and regulate emotions, both within yourself and in others. Here are effective practices to guide you.

1. Practice Mindfulness

Self-awareness is the foundation of emotional intelligence—after all, we can't change what we don't recognize. The more we understand our emotions, the better we can navigate them. Below are key ways to deepen self-awareness, each of which we'll explore further with practical exercises later.

- Regular Check-Ins: Take a few moments each day to pause and notice what you're feeling without judgment.

- Body Scans: Pay attention to physical sensations (tight shoulders, clenched jaw) as clues to your emotional state.

- Present Moment Awareness: Use breathing exercises to stay grounded and aware of your emotions in real time.

2. Build a Vocabulary for Emotions

- Expand Your Emotional Lexicon: Learn and use words beyond basic emotions (happy, sad, angry) to describe feelings like overwhelmed, hopeful, or content.

3. Recognize Emotional Triggers

- Proactive awareness of our triggers is essential for managing emotional responses. Identifying them before they arise breaks the react-regret cycle, allowing for conscious choices instead of impulsive reactions.

Deepening our Emotional range

Expanding our emotional vocabulary is a powerful tool for self-awareness, healing, and personal growth. When we can accurately name our emotions, we gain clarity about our inner experiences. Instead of lumping emotions into broad categories like "positive" or "negative," we develop the ability to recognize subtle differences—distinguishing frustration from resentment, loneliness from sadness, or contentment from fulfillment.

Refining our emotional lexicon is like upgrading from a blurry black-and-white image to a high-definition, full-color picture of our inner world. This precision allows us to navigate our emotions with greater awareness and choice, much like a musician fine-tuning an instrument to create harmony rather than noise. The more words we have to describe what we feel, the better we can understand ourselves, communicate with others, and respond intentionally rather than react impulsively.

Here is one way to organize and understand the emotions, grouped into three main types.

1. Anger-Related Emotions

- Irritated: Mild, ongoing annoyance from repeated small disturbances.
- Annoyed: Slight anger or discomfort from something bothersome.
- Impatient: Intolerance of delays, leading to frustration.
- Frustrated: Upset from thwarted expectations.
- Offended: Hurt or upset by perceived slights.
- Agitated: Nervous anger with physical restlessness.
- Angry: Strong displeasure from perceived injustice.
- Indignant: Anger at unfair treatment, moral righteousness.
- Resentful: Lingering bitterness from perceived wrongs.
- Exasperated: Anger and frustration from repeated irritation.
- Bitter: Anger and resentment from past grievances.
- Disdainful: Anger and contempt, feeling superior.
- Contemptuous: Disgust and anger, deeming someone inferior.
- Hostile: Aggressive anger with desire to harm.
- Enraged: Intense anger, driving action or retribution.
- Furious: Extreme rage, potential for violence.
- Outraged: Heightened anger at deep injustice.
- Vengeful: Desire for revenge from deep hurt.

2. Grief-Related Emotions

- Sad: Sorrow or unhappiness from loss or disappointment.
- Disappointed: Unhappiness when expectations aren't met.
- Lonely: Isolation or lack of connection, with sadness.
- Guilty: Remorse for real or perceived wrongdoing.
- Regretful: Sorrow about past actions or missed chances.
- Yearning: Deep longing for something lost.
- Grief: Deep sorrow from significant loss.
- Hopeless: Lack of belief in improvement, with despair.
- Heartbroken: Profound emotional pain from loss.
- Despondent: Downhearted, tied to prolonged hopelessness.
- Overwhelmed: Emotionally flooded, grief too intense.
- Anguished: Deep emotional suffering or torment.
- Shattered: Emotionally broken from overwhelming grief/trauma.
- Numb: Emotional detachment, disconnection, inertia.

3. Centered-Related Emotions

- Calm: Free from agitation, inner peace.
- Relaxed: Ease and comfort, releasing tension.
- Content: Satisfaction with the present moment.

- Relieved: Lightening of stress or worry.
- Serene: Deep, profound inner tranquility.
- Curious: Gentle awakening of interest.
- Grateful: Appreciation, nurturing positivity.
- Loving: Warmth and compassion.
- Happy: General joy and pleasure.
- Hopeful: Optimism for positive outcomes.
- Confident: Assurance in self and abilities.
- Proud: Self-respect from achievements.
- Excited: Energetic anticipation.
- Inspired: Motivation and creativity from meaning.
- Empowered: Capability and self-agency.
- Euphoric: Intense joy and boundless energy.
- Ecstatic: Overwhelming bliss.
- Transcendent: Uplifted beyond self, connected to greater whole.

These definitions provide a framework for understanding the various emotional states individuals may experience, helping people recognize and process their feelings more clearly.

If we were to add disgust as an emotion category, it would generally involve feelings of repulsion or strong disapproval toward something offensive, unpleasant, or morally wrong. Here's how it could be broken down into various levels:

4. Disgust-Related Emotions

- Disgusted: Revulsion to something physically or morally offensive.
- Disturbed: Unease from something that challenges values.
- Repulsed: Intense aversion, desire for distance.
- Revolted: Strong rejection of something deemed repulsive.
- Contemptuous: Disdain or scorn for something seen as beneath consideration.
- Appalled: Shock and dismay at something morally wrong.
- Horrified: Extreme reaction to something grotesque or disturbing.

Disgust, anger, and grief, while often perceived as negative, serve as vital messengers, providing valuable information about our needs for protection or distance. Disgust may signal a need for physical or moral boundaries, anger often alerts us to perceived injustices or threats, and grief highlights the importance of what we've lost and the need for emotional processing.

Cultivating awareness of the subtle variations within these emotional categories, such as distinguishing between mere irritation and full-blown rage, or between simple sadness and profound anguish, empowers us to make conscious choices about how we respond.

This nuanced understanding allows us to move beyond unconscious and reactive impulses, fostering more intentional and adaptive behaviors. Instead of being swept away by the intensity of these emotions, we can learn to decode their messages, allowing us to address the underlying needs they represent and navigate life's challenges with greater clarity and control.

POWER PRACTICE

Like father, like son. Not surprisingly, I also grew up emotionally clueless. When I first started doing this kind of personal transformation work, I couldn't tell you how I felt because I simply had no idea.

So I used a grid. For a month I carried a timer in my pocket (this was before smart phones), and when it went off at the hour I referred to my grid featuring a list of 20 or so emotions: Am I feeling that? No. How about that? Hmm. Maybe. By the end of the month my EQ had increased significantly.

Use this link (https://soulfulpower.com/conscious-love/emotions-grid/) to access a downloadable **Emotions Grid** as a powerful tool to track and identify emotions throughout the day—an effective way to enhance Emotional Intelligence (EQ). The grid includes a diverse list of emotions, encompassing both uplifting and challenging feelings across a broad emotional spectrum. To integrate this practice effortlessly, set an hourly reminder on your phone. When it goes off, take a brief pause, review the grid, and check off the emotions you're experiencing in that moment. This simple two-minute exercise can significantly deepen your emotional self-awareness over time.

THE EMOTIONAL SEESAW

With the goal in mind of expanding our EQ, here's a way to think of the human emotional experience, adapted from the teachings of my former teacher, Maia Dhyan. We focus on three main types: anger, sadness, and balanced emotions.

On one side of the emotional seesaw, we find anger-related emotions; on the other, sadness-based feelings. At the center lies balance—the space of love, peace, and stability. Emotions are fluid and interconnected: The further we rise on one end, the deeper we must descend on the other. Beneath anger, there is always sadness—the unspoken pain of "I didn't want it to be this way." Once the adrenaline fades, we often crash into grief and regret before eventually finding our way back to equilibrium.

The energy of anger is active, dynamic, moving from lower to higher intensities. However, as we climb the emotional spectrum, the energy becomes increasingly harder to manage. When we get "activated," our voices rise, our physical expressions become more intense, and at the peak, we may act out—throwing objects or, in extreme cases, resorting to violence. This escalating intensity makes it harder to regain control and respond calmly.

In contrast, the scale of sadness reflects varying levels of low or stagnant energy. These range from higher to lower. The further we descend the more inert we feel; by the time we hit the bottom end of the scale we may feel so numb and powerless that even simple tasks like getting out of bed or leaving the couch become overwhelming challenges.

Our goal here is to return to center as quickly as possible.

Emotional Seesaw

Uncovering Your Emotional Hot Buttons

Becoming aware of your emotional triggers is a crucial step in managing your emotional responses. Emotional reactions can be swift and intense—if we wait until we're already triggered, it's probably too late to respond thoughtfully and at choice. The key to breaking the react/regret cycle is to cultivate awareness of potential triggering situations before they happen.

We all have certain people in our lives who seem to push our buttons more than others. With them, it's especially important to stay present and mindful. But beyond individual interactions, there are common situations where we are more likely to get emotionally triggered. Identifying these patterns allows us to approach them with greater awareness, giving us the power to respond rather than react.

There are also certain situations in which we are more likely to be triggered. For example:

- Living stressed and overwhelmed: When we're already stressed, anxious, or exhausted, our emotional tolerance diminishes, making us more likely to be short-tempered and reactive. Even minor annoyances can provoke exaggerated responses because our emotional reserves are running low. One of the oldest acronyms in the addiction recovery world, HALT—Hungry, Angry, Lonely, Tired—serves as a powerful reminder to check in with ourselves. When any of these factors are at play, it's crucial to approach interactions with extra mindfulness, as we're more susceptible to being triggered.

- Feeling unsupported or unseen: If we feel misunderstood or unappreciated, it can trigger feelings of loneliness, frustration, or sadness, especially if we've been longing for validation or connection.

- Being pushed outside our comfort zone: If we're confronted with situations that challenge our sense of safety, identity, or beliefs—especially in high-pressure environments—we may react emotionally. This often occurs in personal, professional, or social contexts where we feel vulnerable.

- Balancing expectations vs. reality: When reality doesn't meet our expectations, disappointment, frustration, or sadness can arise. This happens frequently in areas like relationships, career, and personal goals.

- Missing boundaries: When our boundaries are crossed—whether emotionally, mentally, or physically—we are triggered, often leading to anger, resentment, or a feeling of being overwhelmed

- Experiencing insecurity or self-doubt: When feeling insecure or uncertain about ourselves, we may react with defensive emotional responses to comments, actions, or situations that reinforce those feelings.

POWER PRACTICE

Identifying Your Emotional Triggers

Our emotional triggers hold valuable clues about unresolved wounds, limiting beliefs, or unconscious patterns that shape how we navigate relationships. By bringing awareness to these triggers, we can begin to reclaim our emotional power rather than being controlled by automatic reactions.

1) Journal Your Feelings

- Take note of moments when strong emotions—anger, sadness, frustration, or anxiety—arise. Describe the situation in detail: Who was involved? What was said or done? How did it make you feel?

- Example: You find yourself irritated every time someone cuts you off in traffic. Whether they did it intentionally or were simply unaware, the reality is that your body pays the price—your stress levels spike, your stomach churns, and tension builds. Yes, their behavior may be rude, but if you take a deeper look, you might realize it's not just about traffic. The same frustration arises when someone interrupts you in conversation. Beneath the irritation, there could be an old wound—perhaps a childhood experience of feeling dismissed, unheard, or unimportant. The conclusions you unconsciously formed back then—maybe that your voice didn't matter or that you weren't worthy of being listened to—still echo in these everyday moments, triggering a reaction far beyond the situation at hand.

2) Ask Why: Identifying Patterns

- Go deeper. What situations or people consistently evoke strong emotional reactions? Do you find yourself reacting similarly in different contexts? Are there themes that repeat across your relationships?

- Example: You feel deeply hurt when a friend doesn't text back right away. On the surface, it seems like simple disappointment, but upon reflection, you realize it ties to a deeper fear of abandonment from past relationships.

Emotional Freedom and Healing the Past

The good news is that past trauma and emotional suppression do not have to define us. Healing is possible. Our past may shape us, but it doesn't have to limit the quality of our relationships. By consciously working through past trauma, and acknowledging and processing our emotions—rather than suppressing them—we reclaim our ability to fully experience life, love, and joy.

CONSCIOUS LOVE

Tools like breathwork, journaling, therapy, artistic/creative outlets, and open communication help us release emotions in a healthy way, fostering resilience, emotional intelligence, and deeper connections with ourselves and others.

I have yet to come across a more effective practice for healing past trauma and clearing suppressed emotions than breathwork. This simple yet powerful technique has the ability to bypass the analytical mind and access deep-seated emotional wounds stored in the body. Even therapists recognize its profound impact—many refer clients to me when they hit a plateau in traditional talk therapy, finding that breathwork helps unlock deeper healing and emotional breakthroughs that conventional methods often struggle to reach.

> "OUR WOUNDS ARE OFTEN THE OPENINGS INTO THE BEST AND MOST BEAUTIFUL PART OF US."
> —DAVID RICHO

Emotions are not the enemy—avoiding them is. Learning to navigate emotions consciously leads to greater mental well-being, stronger relationships, and a more empowered life.

BECOMING MORE LIKE CHILDREN

What was once only spiritual teaching—that everything is energy—is now confirmed by quantum physics. Even what appears solid is, at its core, just vibration. Science also tells us that energy cannot be destroyed; it can only change form.

So, all those countless times we suppressed our emotions because it didn't feel safe to express them? That energy doesn't just vanish. We can't simply sweep it under the rug. Instead, it lingers beneath the surface, festering, accumulating, and intensifying until it demands to be acknowledged and released.

Perhaps this is part of what Jesus meant when he taught that we must "become like little children" to enter the kingdom of heaven (Matthew 18:1-3). Think about a two-year-old having a temper tantrum, a total meltdown. A minute later, they are playing as if nothing happened. They allow emotions to move through them like waves—they feel them fully, express them, and return to the moment. They don't suppress or overanalyze what they feel. We adults get into trouble with the emotions because we stuff them. And as we have seen, there's a price to pay for that.

True emotional freedom doesn't come from avoiding feelings but from allowing ourselves to experience them fully and then letting them go. Like children, we can learn to move through emotions rather than being trapped by them.

Embracing Emotional Sovereignty

Other people's emotions are not your responsibility. Their emotions are not your problem. You don't have to take them on, react to them, fix them, manage them, or carry them.

So often, we get caught in the gravitational pull of other people's emotions, feeling as though we must respond, defend, or soothe. But the truth is, their feelings belong to them, just as yours belong to you. You are not responsible for how they feel, just as they are not responsible for your emotions.

Let them have their emotions. Let them express their truth. You speak your truth, and let them speak theirs. There is immense freedom in realizing that you can stand firm in your own experience without being swept away by someone else's emotional storm.

Being the Eye of the Storm

This is where the power of breath comes in. Between the trigger and the response, there is a sacred pause. The breath creates that space, introducing the possibility of choice.

In that fleeting moment between being triggered and reacting, the breath makes choice possible. It allows us to step back, observe, and respond with clarity rather than being hijacked by knee-jerk emotions. But we must be present—fully aware—to see and seize that moment.

Otherwise, we stay stuck in the exhausting cycle of react and regret—that all-too-familiar pattern of saying or doing something in the heat of the moment, only to wish we had handled it differently.

With breath and awareness, we break the cycle. We reclaim our power. And we learn that true mastery of emotions is not about control—it's about presence, choice, and conscious response.

By consciously practicing these techniques, you'll strengthen your ability to understand and manage emotions, enhancing not only your personal growth but also your relationships.

POWER PRACTICE

Reclaiming Your Emotional Boundaries

Take a moment to reflect on a recent situation where you found yourself caught up in someone else's emotional experience. Maybe it was a heated conversation, a moment of tension, or an instance where someone's frustration, sadness, or anger pulled you in.

- What emotions arose in you? Did you feel responsible for their feelings? Overwhelmed? Defensive?

- How did you react? Did you absorb their emotions as your own, try to fix the situation, or shut down?

- Looking back, how did it all play out? Did your reaction help or escalate the situation? Did it leave you feeling drained or empowered?

Now, imagine how you might handle a similar situation differently. What if, instead of getting swept into their emotional storm, you centered yourself with breath and responded from a place of calm clarity? Visualize yourself standing firm, acknowledging their emotions without absorbing them. What becomes possible if you didn't have to react to their emotions?

This practice is about building awareness. The more you notice these moments, the more choice you have in how you respond next time.

CHAPTER 14
THE HEART OF CONNECTION: COMMUNICATING CONSCIOUSLY

CHALLENGE #10: We have not been taught effective, gracious communication.

SOLUTION #10: Strong communication is the foundation of thriving relationships. By cultivating conscious, compassionate communication—listening deeply, expressing ourselves with clarity and kindness, and navigating conversations with emotional awareness—we build trust, understanding, and deeper connection.

WHY COMMUNICATION MATTERS

Most of us never learned how to communicate in a way that builds connection. We were taught math, history, perhaps even how to dissect a frog—but not how to express our emotions, set boundaries, or really listen.

Yet communication is the lifeblood of every relationship. It's how we share our needs and desires, how we resolve conflict, and how we build trust and intimacy. When it's open, clear, and conscious, relationships thrive. When it breaks down, connection erodes and misunderstanding grows.

Research shows that poor communication is one of the leading causes of relationship breakdown. But here's the good news: it's a skill set—one we can learn, practice, and get better at.

This chapter explores the power of conscious communication: a mindful, heart-centered approach that transforms how we relate. With awareness and intention, we can replace old patterns with new ways of speaking and listening that create deeper intimacy, greater clarity, and lasting connection.

THE MOST COMMON COMMUNICATION PITFALLS

Communication isn't just what we say—it's how we say it, how we listen, and how we respond. When we speak with clarity and presence, we strengthen relationships. When we fall into unconscious patterns, we create distance. Let's explore a few of the most common pitfalls:

1. Misunderstandings

Assumptions and lack of clarity cause avoidable conflict. We jump to conclusions, misread tone, or think we know what someone means without checking. A simple habit—like asking for clarification or reflecting back what we heard—can prevent these snowballing miscommunications. And if you want to ensure conflict, continue having difficult conversations via texting!

> "ASSUMPTIONS ARE THE TERMITES OF RELATIONSHIPS."
> —HENRY WINKLER

2. Not Feeling Heard

Few things feel worse than being dismissed or ignored. Invalidation—whether it's being interrupted or told we're "too sensitive"—makes people shut down. Active listening, reflecting back, and validating someone's experience (even if we disagree) builds emotional safety.

3. Bottling Emotions

Some people equate silence with peace. But bottling emotions doesn't make them disappear—it just delays the explosion. Stonewalling and emotional avoidance lead to resentment and disconnection. We need to speak our truth to stay honest and real in our relationships.

4. Defensiveness

When we feel attacked, we defend. But blame and justification shut down real dialogue. Defensiveness creates an adversarial dynamic where no one feels heard. A battle of egos ensues. The antidote? Curiosity and a pause. Approaching a difficult conversation from the perspective of "What can I learn from this?" is far more powerful and will lead to more open communication than "How can I prove I'm right?"

5. Emotional Reactivity

As we have already seen, our reactions often have less to do with the present and more to do with past wounds. When we're unaware of our triggers, we project old pain onto current conversations. Emotional awareness lets us respond rather than react.

6. Criticism

Criticism attacks the person, not the behavior. It often begins with "You always" or "You never," triggering defensiveness and shut down. The ego's job is to defend—so if you want connection, start with "I" statements such as "I feel..." instead of accusations.

By recognizing these patterns, we can begin to shift. The goal isn't perfection—it's presence, which makes choice possible.

Moving Toward Conscious Communication

Conscious communication means showing up with awareness, honesty, and heart. It's how we build trust, navigate conflict, and create relationships where both people feel seen and valued.

The following are some of the building blocks of effective communication.

1) Practicing active listening. Genuinely seek to understand, not just to reply. This means being present, holding space, and setting aside the ego's need to be right. Avoid interrupting, reflect back what you heard, and ask questions to clarify. When people feel truly heard, they open up.

2) Communicating with clarity and compassion. Speak your truth clearly, directly, and with kindness. Again, use "I" statements to take ownership of your emotions and needs—this keeps blame out of the equation and invites connection instead of defensiveness. Be mindful of your tone; words can either build bridges or erect walls. And make sure you express yourself fully. It's easy to share 95% of what we're feeling and leave out the hardest part—the part that actually needs to be said. Don't stop short. The last 5% is often where the real transformation begins.

3) Becoming aware of nonverbal communication. Communication isn't just verbal. Posture, facial expressions, tone of voice, even energy all send a message. A warm smile or open body language builds trust; crossed arms or sarcasm creates separation.

4) Developing emotional self-regulation. We have already established that reacting from anger or fear almost always backfires. Conscious communication means pausing, breathing, and choosing your words from a grounded place. Breathwork and mindfulness help build this capacity.

5) Asking for What You Need. Many people struggle to express their needs—often out of fear of rejection or unworthiness. But unspoken needs don't get met. Speaking up with clarity and confidence isn't selfish—it's essential. And yes, self-confidence is a skill too—and you can get better at it with practice.

Mastering these foundational elements of communication paves the way for more fulfilling, harmonious relationships—whether in love, friendship, family, or work.

THE POWER OF VULNERABILITY AND EMOTIONAL HONESTY

One of the most transformative aspects of conscious communication is the courage to be vulnerable. As explored in Book 1, vulnerability is not weakness—it's one of the greatest strengths we can bring to our relationships.

Emotional honesty—expressing our true feelings, fears, and desires—creates deeper intimacy and connection. It allows others to see and understand us fully, rather than engaging with a guarded or performative version of ourselves. However, vulnerability requires discernment. Sharing openly with someone who has not earned our trust can lead to hurt, while withholding our truth from those closest to us can create emotional distance.

When we pair emotional honesty with assertiveness, we create the conditions for relationships built on mutual respect, safety, and truth—where both people feel seen, heard, and valued.

CONFLICT RESOLUTION AND NAVIGATING DIFFICULT CONVERSATIONS

Conflict is an inevitable part of any close relationship—but it doesn't have to be destructive. When approached consciously, conflict can be a catalyst for deeper understanding, growth, and intimacy. This section explores how to navigate difficult conversations with emotional intelligence, ensuring that disagreements lead to growth rather than disconnection.

- De-escalation strategies— To keep difficult conversations from spiraling, it helps to have tools for staying grounded. This might mean pausing to breathe, choosing words with care, or practicing reflective listening. Recognizing emotional triggers—both our own and others'—allows us to respond rather than react.

- Breathwork and mindfulness— Emotions can run high in moments of tension. Practices like breathwork and mindfulness help us stay present, regulate our nervous systems, and shift out of fight-or-flight.

- Healthy boundaries—Many people struggle with boundaries, either avoiding confrontation entirely or reacting in ways that push others away. Setting boundaries effectively means expressing your needs clearly while still being open to understanding the other person's perspective. It's about creating space for mutual respect without shutting people out or suppressing your own truth.

- Repairs and rebuilding—Even in the best relationships, communication breakdowns happen. It's a safe bet that we are going to make messes going forward. What matters most is how we recover from them. Very likely, we will again react and then regret something we said or did. The difference now is that we now can see and clean up our mess, rather than being stuck in being right for days or weeks at a time.

    Repairing communication requires ownership—acknowledging mistakes, apologizing when necessary, and finding ways to rebuild trust. It also means letting go of resentment, forgiving, and allowing space for both people to be heard, and making a conscious effort to move forward with a stronger, more conscious connection.

- Shifts from reaction to response—Much of unconscious communication is reactive—driven by emotional triggers and old wounds. Conscious communication invites us to pause, breathe, and speak from clarity. The simple practice of taking a moment before responding can completely shift the tone of an interaction—from defensiveness to openness, from disconnection to possibility.

CREATING A CULTURE OF OPENNESS, RESPECT, AND APPRECIATION

Conscious communication isn't just about improving individual conversations—it's about creating an environment where honesty, vulnerability, and respect are the norm. This means fostering a culture where both people feel safe to express their thoughts and emotions without fear of judgment or rejection.

A key component of this is active appreciation. Too often, we focus on what's wrong in a relationship rather than recognizing what's working. Regularly expressing gratitude, acknowledging efforts, and offering affirmations can strengthen bonds and reinforce positive communication patterns. When people feel appreciated and valued, they are more likely to communicate openly and show up with their best selves.

"IT'S HARD TO COMMUNICATE ANYTHING EXACTLY AND THAT'S WHY PERFECT RELATIONSHIPS BETWEEN PEOPLE ARE DIFFICULT TO FIND."
—GUSTAVE FLAUBERT

Long-term Benefits of Conscious Communication

Learning to communicate consciously does more than prevent conflict—it transforms relationships. Over time, it builds trust, resilience, and a sense of emotional safety. It supports honest expression, graceful navigation of challenges, and deeper intimacy.

As we discussed earlier, practicing conscious communication leads to:

- More authentic and fulfilling connections
- Greater emotional security and trust
- The ability to navigate challenges with grace
- A deeper sense of mutual understanding and respect

Ultimately, the way we communicate shapes the quality of our relationships—and, in turn, the quality of our lives. By embracing the power of conscious communication, we create relationships that are not just functional, but truly transformative.

Preparing the Way for Conscious Love

We've explored the foundational role that communication plays in every kind of relationship—from romantic partnerships to friendships to family and even professional dynamics. As we've seen, conscious communication is not just about speaking eloquently or listening attentively. It's about bringing presence, empathy, and intention to our interactions—choosing connection over control, understanding over ego, and authenticity over performance.

This chapter has laid out the practices and mindsets that allow for deeper understanding, emotional safety, and mutual respect. We've seen how vulnerable truth-telling, assertive expression, emotional self-regulation, and heartfelt listening can radically shift the way we relate to others. We've identified the pitfalls that trip us up and the practices that bring us back to presence. Most importantly, we've illuminated the power each of us holds to transform our relationships—one conscious conversation at a time.

When we commit to communication that is compassionate, honest, and clear, we create the conditions where love can flourish—not just survive, but thrive. We stop seeing our relationships as battlegrounds or negotiations and start experiencing them as sacred spaces for healing, growth, and soul-to-soul connection.

And this is the very groundwork for conscious love.

When we communicate consciously, we pave the way for a love that is rooted not in fantasy or dependency, but in truth, depth, and mutual evolution. This kind of love is not always easy—but it is real. It asks for our full presence, our courage to be seen, and our willingness to grow. It invites us into a higher standard of relating—one where we are both deeply held and radically challenged to become the most authentic version of ourselves.

In the next chapter, we take an honest look at what keeps us from this kind of love. We'll shine light on the unconscious patterns and inner blocks that silently sabotage our connections—from fear of intimacy to unresolved past pain, from limiting beliefs to ego defenses that push others away even as we long for closeness.

This is the work of unmasking the barriers to love.

Because before we can fully step into conscious, soul-expanding partnership, we must first understand what's standing in the way—and learn how to move through it with compassion, awareness, and grace.

Let's begin.

POWER PRACTICES

To integrate the principles of conscious communication, it's essential to engage in regular practices that build self-awareness, emotional regulation, and open-hearted dialogue. These daily rituals create space for reflection and connection—allowing you to speak and listen with greater clarity, empathy, and intention.

Daily Check-In Prompts for Partners

Create a safe, open space for regular emotional attunement. These simple questions foster intimacy, dissolve tension, and help partners stay connected.

Ask each other:

- "How are you feeling today—emotionally and physically?"
- "What did I do today that made you feel loved or appreciated?"
- "Is there anything you need from me to feel more supported?"
- "Were there any misunderstandings or tensions today we should talk about?"

Even five minutes of conscious check-in can make a world of difference.

Reflective Journaling on Communication Patterns

Journaling helps you become more aware of your communication habits, triggers, and growth edges. Try exploring these prompts after a conversation or at the end of the day:

- *Did I communicate clearly and respectfully?*
- *Did I feel heard—or dismissed?*
- *How did I handle conflict or tension?*
- *What would I do differently next time?*

Over time, this reflection reveals patterns and empowers change.

Before Tough Conversations… Breathe!

When you're about to have a difficult conversation—with a partner, friend, or colleague—regulating your emotions can completely shift the outcome. This short breathing practice helps center and

calm your nervous system.
Try this:

1) Find a quiet space and sit comfortably with feet grounded.

2) Inhale deeply through your nose, expanding your belly.

3) Hold for a moment at the top of the breath.

4) Exhale slowly through your mouth, releasing tension.

5) Repeat for 3–5 minutes, focusing on your breath and softening your body.

This creates the space to respond rather than react—and to show up with clarity and compassion.

By making these practices a part of your daily rhythm, you build the foundation for conscious communication—fostering deeper connection, greater emotional intelligence, and more empowered relationships in every area of your life.

PART III

UNMASKING THE BARRIERS TO LOVE

CHAPTER 15
WHAT ARE YOUR OBSTACLES TO LOVE?

Whether we are currently in relationship or looking to be in one, the following teaching from *A Course in Miracles* applies: "It's not our job to look for love but to look within ourselves for the obstacles to love."

Let's take a deep breath and let that sink in!

That means that instead of pouring our time and energy into searching for love—often in all the wrong places—we shift our focus inward, dedicating that effort to uncovering and removing the obstacles to love within ourselves. When we do this, love has a way of finding us—often in the most unexpected places and through the most unlikely circumstances. Need proof? Consider how I met my former partner:

We met for the first time at the Honolulu airport, both en route to Kauai. We'd flown there on different airlines from San Francisco, where we both lived. We each had received the trip as a gift; otherwise we probably would not have taken it. He was offered an earlier flight and declined it, since he was being picked up at a pre-determined time. I ran across the terminal to make my connection, and we ended up on the same inter-island flight, sitting next to each other. Waiting for our luggage, we discovered that we were staying less than a mile from each other—and that we had actually met previously some years earlier. And those are just the highlights of a much longer and more complex story—an extraordinary instance of Divine Choreography!

When we have done the work of identifying and releasing our internal obstacles to love, it will come find us, whether or not we feel ready for it at a conscious level. Of course we can do our part and help lubricate the process by staying conscious to opportunities that may present themselves, and aware of the subtle hints of intuition and guidance. It's probably not going to happen while we channel surf on the couch! Overriding our inertia and overcoming our tendency to hole up and hide out, we make ourselves available, stay open, and participate fully.

This reminds me of the joke about the old man who kept pestering God for money. Every single week he'd be begging on his knees: "Please, Lord, help me; things are tight and I really need to win the lottery!" This went on for some time until finally an exasperated God responded, "Johnny! Help me out here! Buy a lotto ticket!"

Subconscious Fears About Relationships

If we have not been attracting a partner or have a pattern of attracting the wrong kind of person to our relationships—thereby ensuring their failure—it's a pretty safe bet that we are at least ambivalent about the whole endeavor to begin with. Our job then, assuming we do want to be in relationship, is first to identify any unconscious fears to being in relationship and then to do whatever adjustments and corrections need to be made to heal, correct, or get rid of them.

Because of past hurts and traumas, family histories, and cultural conditioning, we bring to the table a set of underlying fears and beliefs about ourselves and about relationships that may cause us to subconsciously sabotage them before they even have a chance. For example, we may attract potential partners who are not available in some way—logistically, because they are either married or already partnered; geographically, in that they live clear across the country;

or emotionally, they are unavailable or simply not a match. We may have great physical chemistry but are fundamentally incompatible personality-wise or spiritually. Or maybe we don't share basic values, dreams, and vision in life. We thereby ensure conflict down the road, once the "honeymoon" ends.

Similarly, we may have been on a quest for the holy grail of relationships, in search of that knight in shining armor who will rescue us from our sense of entrapment and life of meaninglessness. Or that impossibly perfect woman who is going to make everything all right: A whore in the bedroom and a saint everywhere else. Perhaps we have been trying to recreate a past lover (or match an idealized image of a parent)—yet another subconscious unhealthy strategy.

> "IT'S NOT OUR JOB TO LOOK FOR LOVE BUT TO LOOK WITHIN OURSELVES FOR THE OBSTACLES TO LOVE."
> — A COURSE IN MIRACLES

As we begin flushing out the particular set of obstacles in our case, the two main areas on which to focus are 1) beliefs about self-worth, and 2) beliefs about the nature of relationships.

CHAPTER 16
WHAT TRULY DRIVES US?

SABOTAGING RELATIONSHIPS: ARE YOU UNCONSCIOUSLY BLOCKING LOVE?

Have you ever felt as though you're drawn to the wrong people, setting yourself up for disappointment in relationships? You're not alone! Many of us fall into patterns of self-sabotage, choosing unavailable partners or sabotaging what seemed like a perfectly good relationship.

But why do we do this? What's really going on? If our relationships are to have a chance of working, we must be willing to look beyond chocolate and flowers and heart emojis to the hidden currents of the heart. Preparing for the heroic journey of conscious relationships entails identifying and changing core beliefs that may be lurking beneath the surface.

THE YOU UNDERNEATH: UNCOVERING CORE BELIEFS

Core beliefs are developed at an early age, sometimes even pre-verbally. They have no basis in reality. They are lies we took on about ourselves, misunderstandings of a very young, malleable, and uninformed mind that did not know any better. Their language is therefore simple: "I'm stupid." "I'm ugly." "There is something wrong with me." "I'm not good enough." "I'm unworthy of love."

I'm a bad person." "I'm damaged goods."

We then spend our lives either providing supporting evidence that these core beliefs are true, or alternatively, doing everything we can to prove the contrary. To illustrate, one of the core beliefs I took on was "I'm not good enough." I spent much of my life overcompensating to prove the opposite, going out of my way to show others—and myself—that I was good enough. I became the 4.0 student, editor of the paper, teacher's pet. Always there was a need to excel. This drive is not necessarily a bad thing and has definitely contributed positively to my life, but the key is the come-from. Are we striving for excellence because of a healthy desire for self-expression, to be the most that we can be, to fulfill our human potential? Or are we driven to overcome deep-rooted and unconscious feelings of inadequacy?

In the latter case, we would always be imprisoned by unconscious drives and behaviors, and nothing would ever be good enough. Had I not addressed and healed this core belief, my search for excellence would have become an endless endeavor. No degree of success would ever fill that bottomless pit or relieve that insatiable need. I cannot be president of the U.S. because I'm naturalized, but if I were elected president of the world, that still would not be enough! Then I'd have to be president of the solar system, then the galaxy, and so on. Had I not healed that belief, I would have continued to be compelled by an endless hunger for more accomplishments, continually trying to prove my worth.

Another downside to that dynamic showed up this way: if I could not be the best at something, I chose not to play. I therefore avoided or abandoned experiences midstream, before I was able to develop competency, and missed out on many activities, such as team sports, that I might have enjoyed purely for the joy of it.

How did I develop such a core belief? I don't recall a particular incident, and I certainly felt loved, valued, and appreciated by my parents. Who knows what messages my young mind heard and misinterpreted? Maybe it had to do with the birth of younger siblings and my overwhelmed mother unintentionally saying something the wrong way. Maybe I perceived at some point my father's unspoken and unconscious discomfort with my differentness. Maybe it was something that mean third-grade teacher said when I was out for three weeks with a childhood illness and fell behind in the multiplication tables. Ultimately, it doesn't matter. What matters is that I healed that and brought choice back into the equation. I can always choose to strive for excellence because I want to, not because of an unconscious need for approval and self-validation.

External accomplishments and validation are fickle and impermanent. As we have witnessed in recent times and throughout history, fortunes, fame, jobs, and property can all be lost in the blink of an eye. Healing those old wounds and correcting our core beliefs result in freedom of expression and make possible a long-lasting sense of fulfillment.

Transcending Our Core Beliefs

Charlie had a pattern of attracting and falling in love with partners who needed rescuing. An intelligent, successful, attractive, and generous man, he is quite a catch. His partners have tended to be attractive, charming, engaging, and inevitably, struggling financially. Charlie has been working hard at identifying, uncovering, and releasing old beliefs about self-worth: "I'm not good enough." "I'm not worthy of an equal partner." "The only way someone would want to be with me is because they need my money or need to be otherwise rescued by me." Charlie's situation also points to the pernicious doubt that subtly eats away at many people with means: Are they with me for who I am or because of my money? The same could be said about beauty, youth, nationality, certain physical attributes, or social status.

How do we free ourselves from these subconscious dictatorial drivers of our behavior? The first step is to take the time to identify our core beliefs. This requires going within, examining life patterns. Because of denial and built-in blindspots we may need a clear mirror—a therapist, life coach, or even a good and capable friend. (One of the benefits of attending a Soulful Relationships retreat is that we dive in quickly and address deep core issues, and then dissolve those through the multiple breathwork sessions. Plus the group setting allows us to see in others what we may not yet be able to spot in ourselves.)

One helpful practice is like peeling layers of an onion. We begin with a more superficial behavior, concern, fear, or belief, and then peel that layer off by asking questions such as: "If that were true, what would it mean or say about me?" or "What's the worst thing that could happen?" Following is a synthesized example of an interaction with a retreat participant:

"I'm afraid to let others see who I really am."
Question: "What's the worst thing that could happen—what might they see?"
"They wouldn't like me."
Question: "And what would that mean?"
"That they might reject me."
Question: "What would that say about you? What kind of person gets rejected?"
"I'm no fun to be around."
Question: "If you had to guess, what's even deeper than that? What is not fun about you that people might reject if they knew about it?"
"That I'm damaged and don't deserve to be loved."

Bingo. Now the participant has a core belief to work on and clear through breathwork. Getting rid of obstacles is key, not just understanding the dynamic but rooting out or dissolving the beliefs. At the very least, becoming aware of them brings in the possibility of choice, so that when that old tendency of self-doubt rears its ugly head again, we can say to ourselves, "Oh! There's that boring and tired pattern coming up again. How do I want to be in this moment in response to what is happening now?"

CONSCIOUS LOVE

In retreats we use a variety of means to help dissolve or at least dislodge the core beliefs and disempower the hold they have had on us. You can create some of these for yourself. Possibilities include:

- Creating a release ritual—releasing to fire, or having a wake and ritual burial for the old belief. How did it serve you? How did it hold you back? What becomes possible for you by letting it go now?

- Creating a guided meditation or ritual experience for yourself, including a letting-go component or reclaiming a lost part of yourself.

- Breathwork. I have yet to find anything more effective for healing past traumas and releasing outgrown beliefs.

- Retreats. One of the unique gifts of attending a retreat is the chance to experience multiple breathwork sessions in a row, allowing for deeper integration and transformation. Beyond the breathwork itself, retreats offer a space to be witnessed, supported, and gently guided toward greater clarity and freedom—all within a nurturing environment surrounded by like-minded individuals who share a sincere commitment to growth and healing.

POWER PRACTICES

Bringing unconscious beliefs into awareness is a crucial step toward transforming your relationships. In this exercise, you'll uncover and examine the deep-seated beliefs that shape your self-perception and influence how you experience love and connection.

Take a few deep breaths, center yourself, and reflect on your beliefs about your own worthiness: What do I believe about my worthiness to be loved? Consider how you view yourself in relationships and in life. Complete the following prompts in a journal.

For example, beliefs about self-worth might include the following:

- I'm not worthy of love.
- I'm not good enough to deserve a peer, an equal partner.
- There is something wrong with me.
- I'm not _____ enough.
- I'm too _____.
- I can't _____. (e.g. live with anyone, be monogamous, etc.—but who says you have to?)
- I will not find someone else if I leave this one, even if we are both miserable and at each others' throats or we have drifted into a comfortable but passionless companionship.

CHAPTER 17
BELIEFS THAT BREAK RELATIONSHIPS

We have been looking at how core beliefs about ourselves—those deeply ingrained narratives about who we are and what we deserve—can shape and sometimes sabotage our relationships. But there's another layer to this: the beliefs we hold about relationships themselves.

Our past experiences, the relationships we witnessed growing up, societal expectations, and even the stories we consume through media all contribute to a set of assumptions about love, partnership, and commitment. Often, these beliefs operate beneath the surface of our awareness, influencing our choices and behaviors in ways we may not realize.

> IF WE SEE LOVE AS SOMETHING THAT MUST BE EARNED OR CONSTANTLY PROVEN, WE MAY FIND OURSELVES STUCK IN PATTERNS OF OVER-GIVING, PEOPLE-PLEASING, OR TOLERATING LESS THAN WE DESERVE.

Some of these beliefs are healthy and empowering, guiding us toward relationships that are fulfilling and growth-oriented. Others, however, can be limiting—creating fear, resistance, or unrealistic expectations that make it difficult to fully open to love. If we believe that relationships inevitably lead to pain, betrayal, or loss of freedom, we may unconsciously keep love at arm's length.

These beliefs become the invisible architecture of our relationships. They shape how we interpret our partner's words and actions, how we respond to conflict, and even what we allow ourselves to hope for in love. They determine whether we enter relationships with curiosity and openness or with suspicion and self-protection.

The good news is that beliefs are not fixed. Just as we once absorbed these ideas, we have the power to challenge and transform them. By bringing awareness to the unconscious narratives running in the background, we can begin to dismantle the ones that no longer serve us and replace them with beliefs that support the kind of love we truly desire.

In this chapter, we will explore some of the most common negative beliefs about relationships—the ones that quietly hold us back—and how to break free from their grip. Because love, at its core, is not something to be feared or controlled. It is something to be experienced fully, with trust, courage, and the willingness to grow.

COMMON NEGATIVE BELIEFS ABOUT RELATIONSHIPS

Love is one of the most profound and fulfilling experiences we can have, yet so many of us unknowingly put up walls to keep it at bay. These barriers often take the form of deep-seated beliefs about relationships—beliefs we may not even recognize but that subtly shape our choices, behaviors, and ability to open our hearts.

Some of the most common limiting beliefs stem from past wounds and the fear of repeating painful experiences. These subconscious fears can create resistance, self-sabotage, or emotional walls that prevent genuine connection.

They may sound like: *If I get into a relationship, I might...*

- *Lose my sense of self.* Many people fear that being in a relationship means sacrificing their individuality—that their needs, desires, and personal growth will take a backseat to the demands of the partnership. If we've been in relationships where we felt overshadowed, controlled, or pressured to conform, we may unconsciously equate love with losing ourselves. This can lead to resistance, self-sabotage, or an inability to fully commit, as we struggle to protect our autonomy while also longing for deep connection.

- *Get hurt and experience emotional pain.* Love requires vulnerability, and with vulnerability comes the risk of pain. If we've been wounded in past relationships—whether romantic, familial, or platonic—we may develop a subconscious belief that love inevitably leads to suffering. To protect ourselves, we might avoid deep emotional connections, keep others at arm's length, or unconsciously sabotage relationships before they have a chance to grow.

- *Re-experience abandonment.* If we've been abandoned—whether physically or emotionally—we may carry an underlying fear that it will happen again. This fear can manifest as clinginess, distrust, or even an avoidance of relationships altogether. The paradox is that in trying to protect ourselves from abandonment, we may inadvertently create the very conditions that push people away.

- *Lose a loved one unexpectedly.* Grief leaves an indelible mark, and the sudden loss of someone we love can create an unconscious belief that love is unsafe because it can be taken away at any moment. As a result, we may hesitate to open our hearts fully, fearing that the pain of loss will be too great to bear. This fear can keep us from experiencing the depth of connection we truly crave.

- *Be betrayed or cheated on.* Betrayal shatters trust, and the pain of being deceived can linger long after the relationship ends. If we've experienced infidelity or deep dishonesty, we may struggle to trust future partners, always waiting for the other shoe to drop. This can lead to hyper-vigilance, emotional distance, or even pushing away love before we risk being hurt again.

- *Forfeit independence.* Many of us take pride in our autonomy and fear that entering a relationship will mean losing the freedom to make our own choices. If we've seen or experienced relationships where one partner's needs dominated, we may hesitate to fully commit, equating love with restriction rather than partnership. This belief can prevent us from embracing the kind of healthy interdependence that allows love to flourish.

- *Feel trapped, engulfed.* Some fear that being in a relationship will mean losing personal space, being overwhelmed by another's needs, or feeling suffocated by constant togetherness. If we've had experiences where boundaries weren't respected, we may develop an unconscious aversion to intimacy, mistaking closeness for a loss of control rather than a source of support and connection.

- *Be taken advantage of.* Love requires generosity, but if we've been in relationships where we felt used, unappreciated, or taken for granted, we may hesitate to give freely again. This fear can create a guarded heart, making us reluctant to trust or open up, even when we encounter relationships that are genuinely reciprocal and nourishing.

> "BETTER TO PUT YOUR HEART ON THE LINE, RISK EVERYTHING, AND WALK AWAY WITH NOTHING, THAN PLAY IT SAFE. LOVE IS A LOT OF THINGS, BUT "SAFE" ISN'T ONE OF THEM."
> —MANDY HALE

The worst part about these beliefs is that they become self-fulfilling prophecies, unconsciously shaping our actions and reinforcing the very same thing we're trying to avoid. When we expect disappointment, we either attract situations that confirm our fears or interpret events in ways that reinforce them.

The good news is that once we bring these unconscious patterns into awareness, we have the power to change them.

Beyond Beliefs: Embracing Soulful Power

This is where Soulful Power comes in. As we explored in Book 1, true power—the kind that is deeply rooted in authenticity, self-awareness, and inner strength—is not about controlling others or proving our worth. It is about standing in our truth, knowing we are whole and complete as we are, and approaching relationships from a place of empowerment rather than need.

When we reclaim our Soulful Power, we no longer look to love to complete us—we approach it as an opportunity to grow, expand, and share the love we have already cultivated within ourselves. Instead of allowing past wounds to dictate our future, we can step into love with clarity, courage, and the deep knowing that it is not something to be feared—but embraced.

This shift from fear to trust, from unconscious reactivity to conscious choice, is what allows us to break free from old cycles and step into the kind of love that is expansive, transformative, and truly conscious.

Power Practice

Uncovering the hidden narratives that shape your relationships is a vital step toward creating healthier connections. In this exercise, you'll explore the often-unconscious assumptions that dictate your relational patterns and influence your experience of love and partnership.

Take a few deep breaths, center yourself, and reflect on the core stories you tell yourself about relationships. Journal your insights and discoveries. For example, common relationship narratives might include:

- Relationships don't work and are doomed to fail.
- Relationships end up in pain, discord, and divorce.
- Relationships are a distraction.
- I will get sucked into and lose myself again in yet another relationship.
- Relationships are a failure if they do not last "'til death do us part."
- Relationships are too hard. Dealing with motives, feelings, manipulation, and power conflicts takes too much work.
- Men are emotionally out of touch, insensitive and threatened by powerful women.
- Women are emotionally out of control, high maintenance, and needy.

CHAPTER 18
THE PARADOX OF RELATIONSHIPS

With these kinds of beliefs and dynamics going on, it's surprising anyone gets into relationships at all ... or that *only* half of all marriages in the U.S. end up in divorce! No wonder some of us give up on relationships and end up asking ourselves: *Why even bother?* Or telling ourselves more strongly: *No way I am ever doing that again!*

Yet, we long to be with that special beloved, which creates inner conflict and cognitive dissonance.

> WE END UP SENDING MIXED SIGNALS, BECKONING WITH ONE HAND TO COME THIS WAY, WHILE WITH THE OTHER WE SIGNAL STOP RIGHT THERE!

By the way, I am not asserting that the beliefs we discussed above are all false. Most have a degree of truth to them. It is true, for example, that many men are in fact threatened by strong women, and that relationships require a lot of work. Chances are good that we will have the experience of feeling hurt or lost in our relationships, especially if we are not well-versed in the language of the emotions or lack a strong sense of self or personal accountability.

Neither am I suggesting that relationships are a necessary or superior path, nor questioning the validity of a personal choice not to be in relationship or to be in one merely for the companionship. What is important, however, is that such a choice is conscious and not driven by repressed fears and unhealed emotional injuries from our past. As we've seen, unexplored these can significantly impact our relationships.

Conscious relationships, the stuff of heroes

Clearly, this level of introspection requires work. It takes courage and can be nothing less than a heroic effort. What we find along the way may not be fun to look at, but unless we are willing to tackle the issues, we will continue repeating the same old and tired patterns.

The work of conscious relationships is not easy, but it's worth it. Left unexamined, our beliefs and fears will become self-fulfilling and often end up attracting the very same outcomes we intended to avoid.

Marsha has an early memory of being frightened in the waiting room of a hospital. She had fallen asleep, waking up at the very moment when her father and grandmother had stepped out to witness the birth of her younger sister, leaving her briefly alone. Later in life, she developed a pattern of "checking out" and avoiding relating in general—one could say as a way of protecting herself from abandonment.

Ironically, though, not facing our fears can ensure the very outcome from which they seek to protect us. Her disappearing acts and lack of communication for days and weeks at a time have sabotaged friendships and relationships. This pattern of pre-emptive abandonment effectively recreates and assures her waking up alone. Thankfully, she has made great strides in this area.

Similarly, Bill clearly remembers being 3 or 4 years old and being left alone at the hospital by his parents, who had to go to work and take care of the other children. He recalls feeling angry and refusing to speak with them for hours, even after being released from the hospital. A few years later, his father was killed in an accident—another profound loss that deepened his bond with his

CONSCIOUS LOVE

mother, driven by the fear that she, too, might leave. This experience set off an unhealthy pattern in his intimate relationships with women, causing him to settle for anything rather than face being alone. A high-powered and successful executive who is consistently able to confront difficult situations in other areas of his life, he nonetheless avoids conflict with women with whom he is romantically involved, subconsciously trying to avoid the possibility of abandonment. Here's the rub though: Because he withholds his authentic feelings and power in relationship so as not to get hurt, his partners end up checking out—in effect abandoning him emotionally. But the harsh truth is that he did the abandoning first, preemptively, by hiding his authentic self. Thankfully, he too, has found a woman who shares his interests and passions, and who is willing to do the work of relationship maintenance.

Choosing Love Consciously

Love, when approached with consciousness, is not about losing oneself or surrendering independence—it is about expansion. It is an invitation to step into deeper authenticity, to give and receive with an open heart, and to rewrite outdated narratives that keep us stuck in fear.

> Yes, love carries risks. But so does avoiding it.

When we block ourselves from love, we also block ourselves from joy, connection, and the full depth of human experience. The real question is: Are you willing to trust that love, when approached with awareness and intention, can be a source of profound transformation rather than pain?

It's not about ignoring the risks—it's about learning how to navigate them with courage, clarity, and conscious choice. When we shift from fear to trust, from unconscious belief to intentional openness, love no longer feels like a threat. It becomes what it was always meant to be: a path to healing, connection, and the deepest truth of who we are.

CALLING ALL HEROES BOOK 2

POWER PRACTICES

Make a list of advantages and disadvantages to being in relationship. This may help flush out reasons why we may be subconsciously sabotaging ourselves, attracting the wrong partners. It is important to become aware of negative beliefs so that we can work with them; they have to be brought out of the unconscious.

Examples:

Positive Aspects of Relationships

- Commitment: Fosters dependability and security.
- Ego Dissolution: Blurs ego boundaries, creating unity.
- Nurturance: Provides care and support.
- Grounding: Offers stability and a sense of rootedness.
- Connection: Cultivates deep, intimate bonds.
- Spiritual Exploration: Enables focused spiritual growth with a partner.
- Resource Sharing: Facilitates shared support and provision.
- Safe Growth: Creates a secure space for personal exploration.
- Predictability: Offers stability and consistent expectations.
- Sexual Availability: Provides consistent physical intimacy.
- Companionship: Offers shared experiences and belonging.
- Encouragement: Provides mutual support and motivation.

CONSCIOUS LOVE

- Lifelong Growth: Enables shared aging and development.
- Unconditional Acceptance: Fosters a sense of complete belonging.
- Romance/Pampering: Offers special treatment and affection.
- Social Approval: Gains acceptance from loved ones.
- Sacred Experience: Creates feelings of spiritual connection.
- Intimate Knowing: Offers deep, personal understanding.
- Nonverbal Communication: Develops intuitive understanding.
- Creative Collaboration: Enables shared creation and projects.

Negative Aspects of Relationships

- Distraction: Impedes focus on work or mission.
- Reduced Social Time: Limits time spent with other people.
- Envelopment: Creates feelings of being absorbed, trapped, or constrained.
- Sexual Limitation: Restricts exploration of other sexual expressions.
- Stagnation Fear: Breeds fear of personal and relational stagnation.
- Self-Focus Impairment: Hinders individual self-focus.
- Personal Growth Limitation: Restricts single-minded personal/spiritual growth.

- Reduced Solitude: Diminishes time spent alone.
- Emotional Triggering: Heightens emotional drama and conflict.
- Schedule Constraints: Ties one to others' rhythms/schedules.
- Dating Restrictions: Eliminates the freedom to date multiple people.
- Increased Responsibility: Burdens one with relational obligations.
- Potential Boredom: Increases the risk of relational monotony.
- Social Conflict: Causes conflicts with friends and family.
- Behavioral Constraints: Restricts individual freedom of action.
- Interpersonal Friction: Creates the need for constant compromise and agreement.
- Romance Decay: Leads to the eventual decline of romantic intensity.
- Self-Sacrifice: Forces the loss of individual identity.
- Relational Failure: Reinforces a belief that relationships inevitably fail.
- Relational Difficulty: Creates the experience of relationships being excessively hard.

PART IV

PAVING THE WAY FOR LOVE

CHAPTER 19
CLEARING THE SPACE

In this section, we turn the page and begin exploring practices and strategies for creating the kind of love that's rooted in trust, self-awareness, and mutual growth. After confronting the barriers—both internal and external—that prevent us from fully embracing love, we can now focus on conscious, empowered ways to cultivate and nourish deep, meaningful relationships.

CULTIVATING OUR CO-OP GARDEN

As we shift from limiting behaviors and unhealthy patterns to empowered actions, the foundation of any lasting relationship is the work we do within ourselves.

This inner work is much like tending to a garden. In Book 1, *Awakening the Soul of Power*, we introduced the concept of the inner garden—a metaphor for the work of psychological and emotional healing. This inner garden, with its potential for beauty, growth, and abundance, requires dedicated cultivation. This involves diligently weeding out the seeds of past pain, cultivating seeds of love and self-worth, and patiently nurturing the fertile soil of our souls with compassion and understanding.

> JUST AS A GARDENER NURTURES THEIR PLANTS, WE MUST TEND TO OUR INNER LANDSCAPE.

Every garden collects weeds over time, and our inner gardens are no different. These weeds represent unresolved emotions, limiting beliefs, and old wounds that crowd out our ability to grow and flourish. By identifying these patterns and gently removing them, we make room for new growth. This may require forgiveness—of ourselves and others—or letting go of stories that no longer serve us.

In most relationships (excluding polyamorous ones), three entities are involved: Human 1, Human 2, and the relationship. Just like the Humans, the relationship also has a life and energy field of its own that requires care, nourishment, and attention. In conscious relationships, we are therefore talking about cultivating three gardens: yours and mine, for which we are each responsible, and then the collective one, which we must tend together.

In other words, we commit to cultivating our own garden. Then we commit to doing the work of cultivating our co-op garden, and keeping clear the space for our communication, a concept derived from my former teacher, Maia Dhyan.

The 'co-op' garden symbolizes the psychological and emotional space where we can be fully present with each other—openly, authentically, with nothing to hide and no need to hold back. It is a common ground for freedom, an oasis for unguarded self-expression—if tended to, that is. When neglected it becomes overrun with the weeds of unspoken resentment, built-up distrust, and suppressed guilt, eventually leaving little or no space to be with each other. Every time we tell a lie, no matter how small, withhold a communication or even sugarcoat one, a seedling sprouts. If we choose to look the other way, in time it will grow into a weed and take over a whole section of our garden.

That is the sacred if unpleasant work of relationships: the space fills up, and must be cleared. It fills up again, and we must empty it. It fills up with all kinds of debris: resentments, hurt feelings, unexpressed anger, guilt, judgments, lies, transgressions requiring an apology, unacknowledged competition. As much as we wish for these weeds to go away, they won't. They fester there and spread like a cancerous tumor devouring healthy tissues. These are the real killers of relationships. They grow until there is too much accumulated stuff in the space, leaving us no way to move about freely, no space to be with each other fully, authentically.

By that point so much bitterness stands in the way that the tension between us becomes palpable, as though it could be sliced with a knife. The only yield from this garden will be barely veiled sarcasm, covert resentment, and volatile communication.

It is much easier to pluck a seedling than to struggle with an old, overgrown bush with deep, gnarly roots threatening to strangle our garden. Better to nip it in the bud! In conscious relationships we are willing to confront challenging and uncomfortable situations, for that is where the opportunities for growth lie. Ignoring the uncomfortable stuff will make it more painful later and, if we wait too long, will suffocate the life out of the relationship.

The further along we are on the path, the more difficult it becomes to coexist with the weeds, and the more aware of them we become: the tiniest pebble of untruth or withholding becomes unbearably uncomfortable. In the children's tale about the Princess and the Pea, the princess was so sensitive and refined—evolved, we could say—that she was kept awake all night by the discomfort of a single pea hidden underneath a dozen mattresses piled atop each other. Similarly, when we learn to pay attention and tune in, we feel the most subtle disturbances in "the Force." The truth is that many of us do, in fact, feel those interpersonal disturbances: We can read between the lines and sense when something is off, when someone is upset or hurt or guilty or sad but stuffing those feelings. Too often we elect not to "go there," in fear of opening a can of worms. Yet, as unappealing as they may seem, worms can be very beneficial to a garden!

With awareness and compassion, and always open to the possibility that we may be projecting, we fearlessly go where we have not dared tread before. As Susan Jeffers teaches in *Feel the Fear and Do It Anyway*, true growth comes not from waiting for fear to disappear, but from moving forward despite it. In service to the relationship, we brave the discomfort and awkwardness. We take the high road, speak the truth, 'fess up our withholds, make apologies and amends, express our hurt or angry feelings. There is no way around this. Sorry! Like most gardens, this work will require fairly constant vigilance, but once we get it to a certain level, it becomes much easier to maintain.

> "LOVE THE WAY THAT YOU CONQUER YOUR FEAR. YOU KNOW HEARTS DON'T BREAK AROUND HERE."
> —Ed Sheeran

Yet, the outcome cannot be guaranteed. Things may have reached a point that professional intervention may be needed, whether by a therapist, spiritual counselor, coach, or neutral friend.

The important thing is that we are now coming at this from a place of free choice, not driven by loneliness, a need for validation, or subconscious insecurities. As whole and complete beings fully responsible for our own actions and happiness, we offer ourselves to the relationship, for the sake of each of our growth and evolutionary processes. We promise to speak our truth even when doing so is uncomfortable, and refuse to allow the smallest withholds to turn into suffocating weeds. With time, love grows and intimacy deepens. With shared victories and challenges, the depth of connection expands. We experience freedom and relief beyond our imaginations.

POWER PRACTICES

Clearing the Space Practices

Healthy relationships require ongoing maintenance—just as we declutter our physical spaces, we must regularly clear the emotional and energetic space between us. Without this, misunderstandings, resentments, and unspoken tensions accumulate, creating distance and disconnection. The following questions serve as a guide to help keep the channels of communication open, honest, and free from emotional debris:

CONSCIOUS LOVE

1) What unspoken feelings am I holding onto? Have I expressed my needs, disappointments, or fears honestly, or am I suppressing them?

2) Is there unresolved resentment between us? If so, where is it coming from, and what would it take to release it?

3) Have I been fully honest in this relationship? Are there things I've been avoiding saying out of fear, guilt, or discomfort?

4) Do I owe an apology, or am I waiting for one? What would it take to offer or accept an apology with sincerity?

5) 5. Is there a pattern of competition or power struggles between us? How can we shift from rivalry to mutual support?

6) Am I assuming the worst about my partner's intentions? Could I give them the benefit of the doubt and seek clarity instead?

7) What is cluttering the emotional space between us? Are we accumulating small grievances instead of addressing them?

8) How can we make space for a fresh start? What conversations, acknowledgments, or actions would clear the air and restore connection?

9) By engaging with these questions, we actively participate in the ongoing work of keeping our relationships open, honest, and thriving.

CHAPTER 20
RECLAIMING OUR POWER IN RELATIONSHIPS

True empowerment in relationships begins within. As explored in Book 1, our first step is to commit to reclaiming our personal power—declaring our intent and standing by it, even when we falter.

The journey from powerlessness to empowerment is not a straight line. At times we may overreact or fall back into old patterns. That's simply part of the process. The key is to pick ourselves up, learn from our missteps, and keep moving forward. We clean up our messes, make amends when necessary, and adjust course without losing sight of our commitment. Even if we have to "fake it till we make it" at times, what matters is that our commitment remains authentic and unwavering—and that in itself is powerful.

Power is rarely given freely; it must be claimed. If we've given our power away in a relationship, no one else can restore it for us—we must do it ourselves, as gracefully and effectively as possible. This doesn't mean becoming aggressive or seeking revenge; rather, it's about expressing our truth with confidence while keeping our hearts open. The goal is self-expression, not retaliation. When we reclaim our power, we inevitably shift the dynamics of a relationship, and others may feel unsettled. Our task is to navigate this shift with clarity and self-assurance, minimizing unnecessary conflict while remaining firm in our truth.

Because ego-driven power plays often stem from overcompensating for deep-seated feelings of powerlessness, self-awareness is essential. We must recognize and dismantle our own egoic tendencies—the need to win, to be right, to control, or to maintain a particular image. This also means letting go of outdated patterns and roles that, while they may have kept us stuck in powerlessness, have also provided just enough of a payoff to keep us trapped.

Take, for example, the old pattern of feigning weakness to attract a rescuer. Can we finally let that go? While this dynamic isn't exclusive to any gender, far too many women still fall into the belief that men are inevitably threatened by strong women. The problem? It's inauthentic. Women are not powerless—far from it. And relationships built on this falsehood are doomed to imbalance from the start, leading to passive-aggressive behaviors, emotional withholding, and other subtle power struggles. Worse still, unresolved power imbalances in partnerships often get passed down, playing out in unhealthy dynamics with our children.

> "THE JOURNEY FROM POWERLESSNESS TO EMPOWERMENT IS NOT A STRAIGHT LINE."

True power in relationships comes from standing in our authenticity—not from playing small, manipulating, or dominating. When we embrace our power fully and unapologetically, we invite others to do the same, creating partnerships that are rooted in mutual respect, honesty, and deep connection.

EQUALITY STRENGTHENS RELATIONSHIPS

Power imbalances are so ingrained in our social structures that we often don't even recognize them in our personal relationships. Cultural conditioning, gender roles, economic disparities, and childhood experiences all contribute to unconscious dynamics in which one person assumes more control while the other adapts, submits, or resists in subtle ways. While these imbalances may seem minor or even natural, they can erode trust, stifle authenticity, and diminish intimacy over time. A relationship where one person consistently holds more power—whether through decision-making, emotional control, or financial leverage—creates an environment where true connection cannot flourish.

How do we create a balance of power in relationships? Those who hold the upper hand may feel they've "won" in a power struggle, but at what cost? Even when we come out on top, the price is often paid in intimacy and connection. If the other person shuts down, withdraws, or feels diminished, any sense of victory is ultimately hollow and self-defeating.

> LOVE CANNOT BE FORCED. SEX CAN BE COERCED, BUT THE HEART CAN ONLY BE INVITED—COAXED, INSPIRED, DRAWN OUT WITH TRUST AND SAFETY, SEDUCED.

After a power struggle, reestablishing this level of trust takes time and effort. The heart needs to feel safe to stay open.

For those who tend to dominate in relationships, it's worth asking: Would intimacy feel more alive if both partners felt truly equal? Would there be more openness, more warmth, more desire to connect? Would the relationship be free of passive-aggressive retribution—subtle sabotage, forgetfulness, sarcasm, covert resentment?

Balancing power isn't about giving up personal strength or becoming a doormat. It's about creating a dynamic where both people feel equally valued, safe, and free to express themselves authentically. At first, loosening control may feel vulnerable—past wounds may resurface or fears of being taken advantage of may arise. And yes, some people, given an inch, will take a mile. But true empowerment in a relationship means fostering mutual trust, not maintaining dominance.

> "THE GOAL IN INTERPERSONAL OR INTERNATIONAL RELATIONS IS NOT REVERSE OR OPPOSITE EXPLOITATION BUT BALANCE."
> —PO BRONSON

When we stop seeing power as a tug-of-war and start seeing it as a shared foundation, relationships become stronger, more fulfilling, and more connected—not just with each other, but with life itself. Balance benefits everyone.

The Courage to Choose Authenticity

When we suppress our power to keep someone else comfortable, we not only betray ourselves but also stunt the evolution of the relationship. And while standing in our truth may filter out potential partners early on, the reality is that anyone threatened by our empowerment likely isn't the right match for us anyway. Choosing authenticity over approval isn't always easy—it can be downright heroic—but relinquishing our power serves no one. Not us. Not our children. Not the world.

All of us—regardless of gender, identity, or orientation—must evolve beyond outdated power dynamics and find new ways of relating. We need solutions rooted in integrity, in soulful power, rather than the ego-driven cycles of dominance, defensiveness, and conflict that keep us trapped—whether in personal relationships or on a global scale. If we don't consciously shift these patterns, we'll continue waging the same battles, over and over, whether in the form of passive-aggressive standoffs or outright war.

Ultimately, reclaiming our power is an inner journey—one between us and our highest selves. It demands a commitment to stop silencing or shrinking ourselves, no matter the cost. No excuses. No justifications. That is what true empowerment looks like.

And yet, this path doesn't have to be rigid or all-or-nothing. We can approach it as practice rather than a high-stakes test. The journey to empowerment can be gradual, even playful. Every time we act from a place of authenticity—standing in our power rather than reacting from fear—we heal not only the present moment, but also the echoes of past situations where we once felt powerless. True power isn't about domination; it's about strength with compassion. It's about saying no when needed—not just to others' expectations, but also to our own egoic tendencies, the instincts that keep us small.

As we've seen in other relationship challenges, when we step into our power, others may resist. Change disrupts the status quo, and those accustomed to an imbalanced dynamic might feel unsettled, even threatened. For this shift to succeed, there must be at least some willingness from the other party to embrace a new, more equal way of relating. But here's the truth: we cannot force anyone to change. They will either evolve with us… or they won't.

Sometimes, reclaiming our power means walking away. It means freeing ourselves—gracefully if possible, but decisively when necessary. The relationship may not survive in its current form. And letting go, allowing that transformation, can be one of the hardest choices we face. But liberation is not for the faint of heart. In many ways, it's easier to numb out, to settle, to self-medicate. But the price of playing small is far greater. The cost of staying in a dynamic that diminishes our spirit is one we can no longer afford to pay.

RECLAIMING POWER WITHOUT LOSING CONNECTION

Stepping into our power is an act of courage—one that inevitably shifts the dynamics of our relationships. Whether we've historically taken up too little space or wielded control out of fear, reclaiming power disrupts the status quo. And with disruption comes resistance.

When we begin to stand in our truth, some people will embrace and support our growth. Others may feel unsettled, even threatened. If a relationship was built on unspoken power imbalances—whether emotional, financial, or psychological—those dynamics don't dissolve overnight. Patterns resist change. But resistance doesn't mean failure; it's part of the process.

This is where many of us hesitate. We fear that reclaiming our power means creating distance, that standing firm in our truth will drive people away. And sometimes, it does. But true empowerment isn't about winning battles or proving a point—it's about honoring ourselves while staying open to connection.

The challenge is to express our needs, set boundaries, and embody our power without closing our hearts. This requires clarity and self-trust, but also grace. If we approach these shifts with defensiveness or reactivity, we only reinforce the very dynamics we're trying to break. Instead, we cultivate a new way of relating—one rooted in mutual respect, honesty, and emotional integrity.

Still, we can't control how others respond to our growth. Some will rise to meet us, while others may withdraw, push back, or try to restore the old dynamic. At this crossroads, we have a choice: shrink ourselves to maintain comfort, or trust that real connection can withstand transformation.

Reclaiming our power isn't just about shifting relationships—it's about shifting the way we relate to relationships. It's about releasing old fears of abandonment, rejection, or conflict. It's about learning to hold our ground without needing to control the outcome. And sometimes, it's about accepting that a relationship may need to evolve—or even end—for us to remain true to ourselves.

Change is rarely easy. But the cost of staying small is far greater than the discomfort of growth. The path forward isn't about force—it's about alignment. And as we'll see in the next chapter, navigating resistance with clarity and compassion is the key to making these shifts sustainable.

POWER PRACTICES

Power Dynamics: Questions for Reflection

Reclaiming our power isn't just about shifting relationships—it's about transforming the way we show up in them. To cultivate healthier, more balanced dynamics, consider these questions:

1) Where do I tend to give my power away in relationships? Do I shrink, over-accommodate, or silence myself to keep the peace?

2) Am I seeking external validation or approval at the expense of my authenticity?

3) How do I respond when I feel challenged or triggered? Do I react defensively, withdraw, or try to control the situation?

4) What fears drive my patterns in relationships? Am I afraid of being abandoned, rejected, or losing control?

5) Am I engaging in power struggles, or am I creating space for mutual empowerment?

6) Do I feel free to express my needs, boundaries, and desires openly? If not, what holds me back?

7) How do I handle conflict? Do I avoid it, escalate it, or use it as an opportunity for deeper understanding?

8) What role does trust play in my relationships? Do I trust myself to navigate challenges without resorting to manipulation or control?

9) If I were to fully step into my power, how would my relationships change?

10) Am I willing to release relationships that require me to betray myself in order to maintain them?

These questions aren't about blame or judgment—they're about self-awareness and growth. True empowerment comes not from overpowering another, but from standing in our truth with clarity, grace, and self-respect.

CHAPTER 21
CHANGE: THE ONLY CONSTANT

In life one thing we can count on is change. In relationships sometimes we grow together and sometimes we grow apart.

Yes, to the ego change is scary, but what is scarier is that another 5, 10, 20 years will go by and we will remain stuck in lives of meaninglessness and imprisoned in relationships that make us miserable and do not support our highest good. Heroes refuse to be held back by fear, and they are willing to slay their own inner demons: fears, insecurities, and self-defeating behavioral tendencies.

Even when we choose to go our separate ways, there is no need for the love to die. We can allow the form of the relationship to evolve. I remain in good terms with and deeply love all my exes. How could I not? These are the people with whom I have shared the most intimate aspects of who I am.

I am so proud and grateful for the way Markus and I handled our separation. We chose the high road of growth and evolution over the form of the relationship, and continue to work things out several years after. We are still willing to do the work of loving, keeping the space clear, of turning the mirror around, and reining in our projections.

The Reality of Change: Navigating Resistance

Change, even when necessary, is rarely smooth. In relationships, it can be especially complex. When one person begins to reclaim their power, set new boundaries, or stand more fully in their truth, the other may not always welcome the shift. Whether out of fear, insecurity, or a desire to maintain control, resistance often emerges—not necessarily as a conscious effort to hold the other back, but as a reflexive response to the unknown.

Many relationships are built on unspoken agreements—patterns of behavior that maintain a delicate balance, even if that balance is unhealthy. When one person shifts, the entire structure is disrupted. Some partners, friends, or family members will recognize the opportunity for growth and rise to meet the change. Others will resist, whether through passive-aggressive behaviors, withdrawal, emotional outbursts, or attempts to reassert control.

This resistance can be unsettling. It can trigger self-doubt, guilt, or a temptation to shrink back into old patterns just to restore a sense of peace. But true empowerment is not about maintaining superficial harmony—it's about standing in our truth while allowing others the space to choose how they respond.

And that's the key: we cannot force someone to change. No amount of convincing, explaining, or compromising can make another person meet us in a place they are unwilling or unready to go. We can invite them, we can model a new way of relating, but the decision is ultimately theirs.

This is where relationships reach a crossroads: they either evolve together or they fall apart. Some will rise to the challenge, willing to grow alongside us. Others may retreat, resist, or cling to the old dynamic. Neither outcome is inherently right or wrong—only an indication of alignment, or lack thereof.

Choosing to stay in a relationship where resistance is strong requires discernment. Is this a temporary discomfort as the other person adjusts, or a deeper refusal to engage in mutual growth? Are they open to dialogue, or do they shut it down? Is there genuine effort toward understanding, or merely empty words?

The reality is that not every relationship can withstand transformation. And that is not a failure—it is a natural consequence of growth. Sometimes, the most loving thing we can do is release what no longer serves us, trusting that in doing so, we create space for relationships that align with who we are becoming.

Change is inevitable. Resistance is natural. But in the end, the relationships that are meant to endure will not require us to abandon ourselves in order to preserve them.

When Love Evolves in Different Directions

Not all relationships are meant to last forever in their current form. When we reclaim our power and step more fully into our truth, some relationships will rise to meet us, while others may falter under the weight of resistance. This is one of the hardest realities of personal growth: sometimes, loving someone means recognizing that the relationship, as it stands, is no longer aligned.

But endings do not have to be battles. Separation does not have to be destruction. Relationships can shift, transform, and even end with grace, respect, and love. When two people can no longer walk the same path, they still have a choice—to part ways with resentment and blame, or with clarity and compassion.

This is the essence of Conscious Uncoupling, a term coined by Gwyneth Paltrow—an approach that honors what was, acknowledges what is, and allows for a transition that serves the highest good of both individuals. Rather than engaging in power struggles, lingering in bitterness, or turning love into war, conscious uncoupling offers a way to release a relationship with intention and integrity.

In the next section, we'll explore how to navigate this process with awareness, courage, and an open heart—transforming endings into opportunities for healing and growth.

> "THERE COMES A TIME IN YOUR LIFE WHEN YOU HAVE TO CHOOSE TO TURN THE PAGE, WRITE ANOTHER BOOK OR SIMPLY CLOSE IT."
> —SHANNON L. ALDER

CONSCIOUS UNCOUPLING

Earlier we explored what it takes to have a conscious relationship. What are the elements of conscious separation?

- Compassion comes from Latin for "feeling or suffering with." It is rooted in:

- Respect is the very least we can extend to each other, having shared the most intimate aspects of our lives. This entails respecting oneself first and foremost, yet also embodying:

- Humility. Knowing that we don't have all the answers, that we are not perfect, and share part of the responsibility. Humility is the basis for:

- Forgiveness. Giving each other the benefit of the doubt, the space to be human and make mistakes. It requires:

- Generosity is built into our cellular structure. It is better to be free than stuck in power struggles about possessions. Generosity makes possible:

- Compromise. Being willing to reach compromise requires:

- Letting go of being right. As the saying goes, do you want to be right or happy?

When separation is approached with intention, integrity, and love, it can be a doorway to deeper personal freedom—not just an ending, but a transformation. Yet arriving at this decision is rarely simple. How do we know when it's truly time to walk away, and when we're meant to stay and do the work? Relationships, like all living things, go through cycles of challenge and renewal. Some difficulties are opportunities for growth, while others signal that the connection has run its course. The key is discerning the difference.

In the next section, we'll explore the questions that help us navigate this choice with clarity—learning to recognize whether a relationship is calling us to deepen our commitment or release it with love.

POWER PRACTICES

Questions for Reflection

Change is inevitable, but when we step into our power, not everyone will be ready to meet us there. These questions can help you navigate resistance—both from others and within yourself:

1) How does my growth challenge the existing dynamics in my relationships?

2) Am I afraid of outgrowing someone I love? If so, what is that fear really about?

3) What patterns of resistance am I noticing in my relationships? Are they subtle (passive-aggressiveness, withdrawal) or overt (arguments, criticism)?

4) Am I expecting someone else to change just because I have?

5) How do I respond when faced with resistance? Do I retreat, push harder, or try to persuade?

6) Am I allowing space for others to adjust, or am I impatient with their process?

7) Am I holding onto relationships that no longer align with who I am becoming?

8) How do I discern between resistance that's part of natural growing pains and resistance that signals an impasse?

9) Am I willing to let go of relationships that can't evolve with me?

10) How can I honor my own growth while still allowing others to move at their own pace?

Navigating resistance isn't about forcing others to change—it's about staying true to your path while allowing space for those around you to choose their own.

CHAPTER 22
STAYING IN THE CAULDRON

'TIL DEATH DO US PART?

The question of how long to stay in a relationship is one of life's most profound and challenging decisions. Love is often romanticized—seen as something that should always feel blissful, effortless, and expansive. But every relationship inevitably moves past the initial euphoria into the reality of day-to-day life.

As we explored earlier with Peck's definition of love, when challenges arise, the instinct for many is to think, *I'm outta here!* The "grass is greener" syndrome may kick in, making single life—or someone else's relationship—look far more appealing. But once we understand the difference between the feeling of love and the act of loving, we gain the ability to make a conscious, grounded choice about whether to stay or go.

Sometimes, walking away is the highest choice. Not all relationships are meant to last "'til death do us part," and leaving doesn't necessarily mean failure. Maybe, after the honeymoon phase fades, we realize there's little substance beyond physical attraction. In such cases, moving on can be an act of integrity.

At other times, staying is the wiser path—not out of complacency, but with intention. It means actively engaging, observing the signs, listening to our intuition, and leaning into the discomfort rather than fleeing at the first sign of difficulty. Relationships are crucibles for growth, and when we allow ourselves to stay present through the heat of transformation, we create space for deeper healing and connection.

That said, I want to be clear: I am not advocating staying in abusive relationships. If there is harm, manipulation, or control at play, seeking professional support is crucial. Authorities may need to be involved, and there are organizations that provide protection and guidance in these situations.

Barring those extremes, how do we know whether to stay or go?

Is Growth Happening?

Relationships are not meant to be a constant high. They ebb and flow, cycling through moments of deep connection and inevitable challenges. That's the nature of any meaningful relationship—whether romantic, familial, or even professional.

But how do we know when it's truly time to go, rather than just another opportunity to grow? If we're not making decisions based purely on fleeting emotions or temporary discomfort, what is the measure?

The answer is different for all of us. All relationships have ups and downs, and just because it's going through a rough patch doesn't necessarily mean it's time to bail. For me, it comes down to one guiding principle: Is growth happening? In other words, both partners are committed to their own and each other's growth above the form and structure the relationship may take as it evolves.

> COMMITMENT TO GROWTH IS PRIMARY, OVER AND BEYOND THE CONTAINER, THE SHAPE, OF THE RELATIONSHIP.

My ex and I chose to part ways when we realized that the container of the relationship was beginning to interfere with each of our growth. The love and passion were still there. Sometimes the highest—and certainly not the easiest—choice is to walk away even when the feelings of love and passion are still alive. Yes, this is tough. It's heroic. But who said that longevity is the only measurement of the success of a relationship? For me the important measurement is whether the relationship is supporting its partners to evolve spiritually, to become better, more compassionate beings. Is it prodding them to fulfill their human potential?

Conversely, relationships that stifle growth, compromise well-being, or are maintained out of fear should be reassessed. The key is self-honesty and recognizing that love should be a catalyst for growth, not a prison. When growth is present, leaning in is warranted. When absent, courageous departure may be the most loving act.

It can be helpful to work with professionals and build a strong support system as you figure this out. Breathwork might also bring some clarity.

Ultimately, the decision of how long to stay in a relationship is deeply personal, shaped by our values, level of growth, particular situations, and evolving understanding of love. When commitment to growth—both personal and mutual—takes priority over the shape of the relationship, we gain clarity and freedom to choose what serves our highest good. Whether we choose to stay and lean into challenges or decide to part ways with compassion, what matters most is approaching the journey with intentionality, raw honesty, and a heart aligned with growth.

Georgina's Journey: A Case Study

Georgina knew, deep down, that her lover was not her equal. She did not question his worth as a person, but she couldn't ignore the disparity between them—his emotional availability, spiritual depth, and level of self-awareness simply did not align with hers. His life was still somewhat unsettled in the wake of addiction recovery, yet an enticing business breakthrough loomed on the horizon. She wrestled with the uncomfortable question: Was she staying out of love, or was she selling out to the promise of financial security and her own longing to be taken care of?

Through coaching and breathwork, another layer emerged—her deep sense of responsibility and guilt. He had once threatened suicide if she left, a heavy burden that had kept her tethered to the relationship. Was she unconsciously reinforcing his dependency to validate her own self-worth? The realization unsettled her.

Peeling back the layers even further, Georgina traced these patterns to an old wound—her father's absence after her parents' divorce. She had carried a deep sense of abandonment, a silent ache she hadn't fully confronted. But it didn't stop there. As we delved deeper, a buried trauma surfaced—an incident of sexual abuse by a neighbor in her pre-teen years. It was yet another betrayal, another wound inflicted by a man, compounding her disappointment in her father's inability to protect her.

With courageous vulnerability, Georgina faced her shadow. Through breathwork, she processed the pain, releasing the lingering shame and feelings of unworthiness that had shaped her choices in relationships. Healing those wounds shifted everything. Today, she is with a partner who meets her on equal footing—spiritually aligned, financially successful, and most importantly, committed to doing the deep work of conscious relationship. Together, they navigate the path of trust with mutual respect, co-creating a love that is conscious, empowered, and free of past entanglements.

> "THERE IS NO REMEDY FOR LOVE BUT TO LOVE MORE."
> —HENRY DAVID THOREAU

How committed are you to your full and authentic self-expression—no matter what? Remember: what is true, what is of love, what is in the mind of God, will be there on the other side of our leap to freedom.

POWER PRACTICES

Here are some key questions to help navigate the choice between staying and leaving with clarity:

CONSCIOUS LOVE

Assessing the Health of the Relationship

1) Does this relationship bring out the best in me? Do I feel seen, valued, and respected?

2) Do we share core values and a vision for the future, or are we fundamentally misaligned?

3) Are conflicts opportunities for growth, or do they follow the same unproductive patterns?

4) Am I staying out of love and mutual commitment, or out of fear, guilt, or obligation?

Checking in With Your Inner Self

1) Am I being honest with myself about what I need and how I feel?

2) Do I consistently feel safe, supported, and at ease in this relationship, or am I often walking on eggshells?

3) Have I expressed my needs clearly and been met with openness, or has my voice been dismissed?

4) Am I shrinking, compromising my truth, or betraying myself to make this relationship work?

Understanding Patterns and Growth

1) Have we both done the work to heal and evolve, or is one of us carrying the emotional labor?

2) Are past wounds and fears keeping me here, or is this relationship truly aligned with who I am becoming?

3) Is there still mutual curiosity, care, and effort to deepen the connection, or has it become stagnant?

Considering the Impact of Leaving

1) Do I feel more fear about the unknown than clarity about what is right for me?

2) Am I willing to face the grief of letting go in order to create space for something healthier?

3) If I knew I would be okay—emotionally, financially, spiritually—would I still choose to stay?

4) What would I tell a dear friend if they were in my situation?

The answers to these questions won't always be immediate or easy, but they offer a powerful starting point for uncovering the truth. Whether the path leads to deeper commitment or a conscious uncoupling, the most important thing is to honor yourself, your growth, and your deepest knowing.

CHAPTER 23
NAVIGATING THE LOVE FRENZY

Now that we understand the difference between being in love and the act of loving, how does that help us navigate those times when we are in the throes of love's intoxicating bite, when we get caught up in the Love Frenzy?

First of all, allow yourself to enjoy the spell; stretch it as long as you can. Being in love, and having it reciprocated, is one of life's most intense, joyful, and ecstatic experiences. But as we all know, it is not only that. With the peaks come the valleys: confusion, self-doubt, pining away, suffering. For some, such "sweet suffering" is part of the experience of being in love, but it can drive us to extremes.

How do we maintain equanimity and peace of mind when in the throes of love, when the object of desire does not return a phone call or pull back in some other way?

Buddhism teaches that the root of suffering is desire, which is often interpreted as attachment. What is relevant to this discussion is that we are attaching to outcome, to things turning out a certain way. We are also attaching to a specific person. Very likely, we have sent out and secured little energetic feelers or tendrils with suction cups that attach to others. Hence the suffering when they don't return our affection as we had hoped.

Even those of us who feel complete and whole and who—at the conscious level at least—know that there is not another person out there who can fulfill us, can still be triggered and have insecurities surface when under the spell of love. Is this not a relinquishing of power?

Yet, detachment is not the answer. It might sound like semantics, but detachment implies a cool, aloof and protected state, perhaps even a closed heart. What we are striving for, rather, is a state of nonattachment. Our commitment is to keep our heart open, no matter what—with hands off and reeling back our suction cups—standing free and allowing everyone else to do the same.

No doubt: this is easier said than done. This is where the rubber meets the road.

What do we do when we want to maintain a sense of center and be in charge of our life, not ruled by out-of-control hormones and other people's actions and reactions? How do we navigate The Love Frenzy—when that almost uncontrollable, all-consuming desire arises in us to pick up the phone, fire off that text or email, or drive by their house to see if they are home? Or, for that matter, when the seemingly irrepressible desire for a cigarette, or a line, or a bump, or that compelling craving for a little something sweet, or that compulsive need to check email first thing in the morning?

- Stop what you're doing. Go for a short walk. Whatever it is you crave will be there in five or 10 minutes if you still choose it. The point is, let it be a choice, rather than blindly reacting to brain biochemistry or unconscious impulses. If we are going to make a certain choice, let's at least do it as consciously as possible.

- Breathe deeply. This helps when you find yourself pining away, longing for something.

- Explore and question. Ask yourself: What is going on underneath the desire to call? What am I feeling right now? What am I feeling when I find myself longing to be with them, wishing that they would call me? (Am I feeling, for example, stressed out, tired, lonely, anxious, jealous, unappreciated?) If I am feeling disconnected, what am I really longing to connect with?

- Feel. Be willing to feel the longing, to drop down into the body, way down into the gut. Be willing to feel the discomfort and not numb out to it. If you focus on it—is there anything lurking underneath? Feelings of inadequacy? Old fears of rejection or subconscious memories of abandonment? Be willing to feel and have emotions surface. Give them voice: cry, scream, sing, journal. Feel the frenzy . . . and choose. What is the highest thing I could do right now?

- Remember. Make a conscious effort to remember who you are. Remember the commitment to keep the heart open, no matter what—again, not in a door-matty sort of way, but with self-respect and self-honoring.

- Evoke gratitude. Focus on the positives in your life.

- Take a bath. Relax.

- Try breathwork. It's the most effective tool I know of to access and clear past trauma as well as regain a sense of center and perspective.

- Connect; resist the tendency to isolate.

- Distract yourself: When in doubt, sometimes I go to the movies! Getting lost in another world for a couple of hours sometimes gives me the necessary distance and perspective I needed. Netflix therapy is indeed a thing.

"LOVE IS AN UNTAMED FORCE. WHEN WE TRY TO CONTROL IT, IT DESTROYS US. WHEN WE TRY TO IMPRISON IT, IT ENSLAVES US. WHEN WE TRY TO UNDERSTAND IT, IT LEAVES US FEELING LOST AND CONFUSED."
—PAULO COELHO

CHAPTER 24
CLEARING THE PATH TO LOVE

As we move forward in this journey of conscious love, by now we are clear that the path to deep, meaningful relationships begins within. The work we've done here—reclaiming our personal power, shifting old paradigms, and clearing the space within ourselves—isn't just about preparing for love, it's about cultivating a love that is sustainable, authentic, and transformative.

Paving the way for love requires us to let go of the myths and unrealistic expectations we may have carried from the past, to recognize the power dynamics that can distort our relationships, and to understand that true intimacy is rooted in balance, trust, and mutual growth. As we have seen, relationships are not about controlling or forcing an outcome but about inviting connection, fostering understanding, and embracing change as part of the natural flow.

The practices we've explored—whether it's reclaiming our power, challenging the myths we hold about relationships, or envisioning the kind of partner we truly desire—are all tools that help us clear the space for love to enter. By understanding what we truly seek, becoming aware of what no longer serves us, and being willing to release attachment to rigid outcomes, we create fertile ground for something more expansive to emerge.

Letting go doesn't mean giving up; it means making room for what's truly meant for us. Whether it's about shifting the dynamics in an existing relationship or stepping forward into a new chapter, the process of paving the way for love is ultimately about staying open, conscious, and grounded in our truth.

ENVISIONING LOVE

Years ago, during a period between relationships, I found myself on the Hawaiian island of Kauai. There, I visited a Hindu temple that housed a stunning crystal, towering about four feet high. Each day, monks would gather the written prayers left at the base of the crystal and offer them to the fire. Inspired by the sacred energy of the space, I decided to create a list of qualities I wanted in a partner—without judging whether it was trivial or profound. A year later, after entering a new relationship, I stumbled upon a copy I had made of that very list. I was amazed to see how many of those qualities had manifested. There is real power in dreaming, getting clear about our desires, and putting them out into the universe!

As we close Part 4, remember that love is a living, evolving practice—one that requires conscious effort, but also deep trust in the process. You've already begun paving the way. Now, it's time to step forward with intention and grace, knowing that the love you seek is already on its way.

POWER PRACTICES

Dreaming Up Your Love

Step 1. Before we can cultivate a conscious, fulfilling relationship, we must first become clear on what we truly desire. Again, you may find it helpful to create a list of qualities you seek in a partner—everything from values and emotional availability to shared interests and communication styles. What's important to you? Be specific.

Here are some aspects to consider:

- Core values: Integrity, honesty, kindness, loyalty, respect

- Emotional Availability: Openness to sharing feelings, emotional maturity, empathy

- Communication style: Ability to listen, willingness to communicate openly, non-defensive

- Compatibility: Similar life goals, vision for the future, lifestyle preferences

- Interests and hobbies: Shared passions, mutual interests, willingness to explore new activities together

- Conflict resolution: Ability to handle disagreements respectfully, avoid drama, resolve issues with compromise and understanding

- Supportive nature: Encouragement, understanding during challenges, shared responsibilities

- Physical attraction: Mutual chemistry, physical closeness, and connection

- Independence: Respect for personal space and individuality, ability to maintain independence within the relationship

- Sense of humor: Ability to laugh together, enjoy playful moments, and keep things lighthearted when needed

- Shared spirituality or beliefs: Similar spiritual practices, respect for each other's beliefs

- Family and relationship dynamics: Compatibility in how we relate to family, respect for boundaries, and family priorities

- Trustworthiness: Dependability, honesty in actions and words, transparency

- Generosity and giving: Willingness to give, both emotionally and practically, within the relationship
- Adaptability: Flexibility in handling life changes and new challenges together
- Respect for boundaries: Healthy understanding and respect for each other's limits, space, and needs

These qualities help create a clear vision of what you want, and can also serve as a guide for assessing potential relationships.

Step 2. Next, take it a step further: mark which qualities are non-negotiable and which are flexible.

Step 3. Once you've put your vision into words, release it. Ritualize the letting go. Burn the list, bury it, or offer it to the wind. This act symbolizes surrender, reminding us that while clarity is essential, attachment can be limiting.

Having said that, the process of getting clear tends to be catalytic! True love often arrives in ways we least expect, and by creating space for possibility, we invite something even greater than what we imagined. Are you ready for love?

PART V

SACRED UNION: MERGING SEXUALITY AND SPIRITUALITY

CHAPTER 25
HARMONIZING SEXUALITY AND SPIRITUALITY

Like earthquakes, hurricanes and volcanoes, sex is a force of nature. When unharnessed, sexual energy can be life-giving, ecstatic, and transformative. However, when unhealed and expressed unconsciously, it can wreak havoc and destruction. Repressing or ignoring it does not work. When we attempt to control or suppress sexuality, it often finds expression in unhealthy and harmful ways.

What is it that makes sexuality such a powerful force? Surely it is more than just an out-of-control biological trick—the instinct to procreate gone awry! We want it. We must have it. We obsess about it. Entire industries exist to increase our chances of "getting some." Sexual passion has fueled art, music, and literature since time immemorial, and undergirds many a modern industry: cosmetics, fashion, health clubs, plastic surgery, romance novels, entertainment, advice columns, self-help, wedding and honeymoon travel. We adorn ourselves with houses, cars, jewels, and clothing like the plumage of birds in heat—making ourselves bigger, more colorful, and attractive in order to get laid. Annual global revenues from the perfume industry alone are estimated at $55.5 billion.[9]

Entire identities are built around it: Sex can validate or destroy our egoic self-image. It can lead to ecstatic states of union and connectedness, even self-transcendence, or it can leave us feeling lonelier and emptier than before. When it clicks, time stops.

Union, bliss, and a sense of oneness ensue, all parties feeling empowered and renewed. When it doesn't, bruised egos and even insane behavior can erupt. Twisted aberrations of love and lust drive people to suicide and homicide.

Sex has engendered some of the most beautiful art in human history—and some of the most horrific crimes. I have witnessed people in their 70s and 80s regress to childish teenage behavior when in the throes of lust, and otherwise conscious, empowered, and spiritually evolved people lose their emotional balance or risk their health over sex.

From revered spiritual teachers whose hidden liaisons shattered the trust of their followers to powerful financiers who procured women and children for the sexual exploitation of themselves and their elite circles—sexuality, when misused, has the potential to destroy lives, tarnish reputations, and dismantle legacies.

Sex almost brought down a presidency and has been the cause for the implosion of many a political or religious leader's career. Queens have lost their heads and kings abdicated their thrones over it. People become unhinged, such as the astronaut who drove from Texas to stalk her ex in Florida, wearing adult diapers so she could avoid having to make bathroom pitstops.

It can all feel confusing, unpredictable, and even dangerous. Sex devoid of mindfulness and divorced from the sacred lends itself to abuse of power, addiction, and other unhealthy expressions.

This is the landscape we've inherited, but it doesn't have to define our future. Perhaps it's time to challenge our assumptions about sex altogether.

CHAPTER 26
SACRED SEXUALITY ... AN OXYMORON?

For some people, "sacred sexuality" is an oxymoron, an inherent contradiction in terms. And it's no wonder, given humanity's religiously-inspired history of making sex wrong. Yet, if you doubt the connection between sexuality and spirituality, just ask yourself: whose name is most commonly invoked at the point of orgasm?

Before I was exposed to spiritual practices such as meditation and conscious breathing, the only time my mind would cease its endless chatter was during sex. In those moments I was able to go beyond myself, transcend my inner dialogue and self-doubts, and become one with another. Time stopped. In French, orgasm is referred to as *la petite mort*, the little death. For at that moment there is a collapse of the ego boundaries that keep us apart; we dissolve into ourselves and each other in an exquisite state of timelessness, feeling at one with each other and with everything. We die briefly to our separate identities, our ego selves, attaining a state of ecstasy as we are lifted out of ourselves.

With the emergence of the patriarchal cultures and religions about 6,000 years ago, the physical and the spiritual were split. God was disembodied and exiled to the realm of the abstract, and heaven was pushed away from the Earth into the far reaches of outer space. Where the hell is heaven anyway? The spiritual became inscrutable, remote, disembodied—an asexual force, disconnected from the sensual world. It is telling that my computer's thesaurus lists "spiritual" as the antonym of "sensual."

After the split, anything associated with the physical, including the Earth, became inferior, less than perfect—something to be conquered, subjugated, and controlled. No wonder we treat our "godforsaken" planet the way that we do. The human body? Animalized. And sexuality? Sinful, dirty, even demonized. So of course we have sexual issues!

This regrettable, tragic situation has not always been the case. Back when the Goddess was revered, this false dichotomy was not the prevalent belief. Even more recently, in the East, Tantric, and Taoist spiritual traditions did not consider sexuality and spirituality to be separate and at odds. Sexuality was considered not only sacred but as a powerful vehicle to the divine.

In Hinduism the Kundalini energy, which, when ignited, rises up the spine to bring about enlightenment, is also the sexual energy. And to most indigenous and shamanic traditions everything is sacred, including trees, rocks, animals, clouds … and the sexual organs.

What's more, the major Western religions teach that God is omnipresent, all-pervasive, infusing all of existence. To think that God is somehow absent from the most intimate aspects of our humanity, that "everywhere" excludes the genitals and the bedroom, is illogical and absurd. Either God is omnipresent, or God isn't.

The problem with the strategy of reducing sexuality to a necessary evil and attempting to limit its purpose to reproduction is that, simply, that does not work. We now know from physics that everything is energy, and that energy cannot be destroyed. Therefore, what we try to suppress here is going to emerge there eventually, and, unfortunately, too often in unhealthy expressions.

The price we pay for suppression? The global sex abuse crisis in the Catholic Church. The innumerable sex scandals in the lives of politicians, coaches, and spiritual leaders. Not to mention an unfathomable number of broken relationships, a disturbing palette of sexual dysfunction, who knows how many psychosomatic symptoms caused by sexual frustration, and countless lives of unnecessary misery, unfulfillment, and inner torment. Humanity is a sexual mess! We are truly *obsexed*.

The more we try to suppress, ignore, or control sexuality, the more it grips our attention: in the media and entertainment, in literature and the arts, in the lives of our celebrities, in our own lives. And everywhere we look sex is being used to sell anything from tooth paste to insurance.

Like me, countless others have attempted to reject their inherent, vibrant, and expansive spirituality, confusing it with external, dogmatic, and limiting religious beliefs. Tragically, too many have also tried to push down or ignore their sexuality. It is crucial that we reclaim and learn to reconnect these two integral aspects of being human.

As we have seen in Book 1, integrity refers to wholeness. It is impossible to be whole beings as long as we keep rejecting any part of who we are. Reclaiming and reintegrating all parts of our rejected humanity is necessary in order to become whole again, and more fully human. We need to sacralize our humanity and reconcile our sexuality and spirituality. We need to reclaim a sense of the sacred in our bodies and in the bedroom.

CHAPTER 27
READY TO BRING SPIRIT INTO SEX?

In earlier times, dedicating ourselves to the sacred often meant withdrawing from the world into monasteries or ashrams. Today, the call is different: We are being called to integrate the sacred into every aspect of our lives—in the boardroom and the bedroom, while stuck in traffic, and standing in line at the grocery store. As we do that, we become more complete whole beings and our lives begin to flow more easily, as if magically.

How do we then begin to bridge the split between these two fundamental and intrinsic parts of our humanity? Bridging the sex/spirit divide is not about inviting into our bed an anachronistic old man with a beard and long white robes, accompanied by a choir of harp-playing cherubs (unless you are into that sort of thing, of course!), nor does it mean having to do it in the missionary position while singing Kumbaya.

No, sacred sex is not boring or staid. Think of it like this: Former porn star and artist Annie Sprinkle compared levels of sexuality to food. Most people, she argues, are having "junk sex"—readily available and superficially pleasurable, but ultimately unfulfilling, like junk food. Then there's health food, requiring more thought and knowledge, like reading labels and shopping at certain aisles in the grocery store. The health benefits of sex are well-documented, from better sleep and stress reduction to improved cardiovascular and immune function. Keeping the pipes clean, so to speak, is good for the body's plumbing, and a good lay can do wonders for our emotional well-being! Finally, there's "gourmet food," demanding knowledge, care, and preparation. Presentation matters.

This is the level of sacred sex. It takes more effort than a quick "Wham, Bam, Thank You, Ma'am (or Man)," but the result is an exquisite, sumptuous, ecstatic experience.

We long for freedom. Sex not only offers a natural high as endorphins flood and titillate our nervous system, but it also provides a respite from the tyranny of our minds.

When we engage in sacred sex consciously and with intention, the possibilities are limitless: self-discovery, self-transcendence, a profound experience of ourselves, and the opportunity to see the sacred in another. At this level, sexuality becomes a powerful force for healing and transformation.

Sacred sex is the kind of love-making that leaves the body convulsing in paroxysms of pleasure, that ecstatically produces an out-of-mind state of transcendence and an expansion of consciousness. It's about the awe-inspiring, mind-blowing, toe-curling kind of sex that erupts in a spontaneous "Oh, God!" from the depths of our being and brings tears of gratitude to our eyes as it animates our body with the holy breath and the sacred fire of love. It is the kind of sex that provides an opportunity for us to feel the depth of our surrender in the very cells of our body, culminating in waves of spasms that slowly subside as we dissolve into glassy tranquility and the heart of perfect stillness.

So, how do we bridge the chasm and bring the sacred into the bedroom? What qualities do we need to cultivate to bring Spirit into sex? Perhaps ironically, we can also think of this following section as: "Nine steps to becoming better lovers."

> "COME SLEEP WITH ME: WE WON'T MAKE LOVE, LOVE WILL MAKE US."
> —JULIO CORTÁZAR

CHAPTER 28
SO YOU WANT TO BE A BETTER LOVER?

Clearly, you are ready to bridge the sex/spirit divide; otherwise, you wouldn't still be reading this. Here are some ways that will help.

1) Reframing sex and spirit. The first step to reconciling sexuality and spirituality is exactly what we have been doing: Upgrading our thinking, cleansing our perceptions, and evolving new belief systems about sex. It's time to upload a new version, for the old system is outdated and ineffective. This entails cultivating our own garden of beliefs, plucking weeds of conditioning and culturally ingrained sex negativity as we plant new seeds such as: "Becoming a better lover is a spiritual thing."

2) Sacralizing the space. Much of this work, as with other spiritual practices, has to do with the intention that we bring to it. Whatever we can do to set a different tone and bring out the experience of love-making from the mundane will help. In other words, make it special. Ritualize it. Prepare the physical space with things that create a sensual and ethereal mood—candles, scents, the right music. Turn off the TV and maybe cover it with a beautiful fabric. You might even incorporate a ritual bath

and anointing of the body with sacred oils.

3) Going within is sexy. We have already established in Book 1 the importance of going within. All spiritual traditions speak of this in some form. Jesus said the kingdom of God is within. The goal of Buddhist and Hindu meditation is learning to go within and tapping into who we are underneath the chattering of the ego, the monkey mind. The old teaching holds true: The only way we can truly love another is to love ourselves. And the only way to do that is to know ourselves. Going within means both a regular practice and also as a way of preparing for the immediate experience of love-making: Taking even a few minutes to connect, to invoke the presence of the sacred, and to offer ourselves as conduits of love.

4) Honoring your body: A new commandment. The Greek word for temple is *temenos*—something that contains within it the divine presence. Remind yourself of that as you are making preparations. When we treat our bodies as temples of the divine, with the reverence they deserve, we watch what we put into them and the situations in which we place them. We also honor our partner's body with that same reverence. What a difference this simple act of remembering and awareness—even done unilaterally—will make, and what a powerful effect it will have on our sexual experience!

5) Practicing Namaste in the bedroom. Namaste is much more than a nice word we use along with prayer hands and a gentle bow at the end of yoga class. Namaste is a radical concept, one of those handful of spiritual principles that, if we actually embodied and put them into practice, would change immediately our lives and our world. If the sacred in me sees, honors, acknowledges, and bows to the sacred in you, how can I steal from you, lie to you, cheat on you, rape you, allow you to go

hungry, kill you, or invade your country?

What if we extended the concept of *namaste* into the bedroom? The sacred in me sees, honors, acknowledges, bows to—*and makes love with*—the sacred in you. We honor the sacred in our partner. Through our partner, we are actually making love to God in this realm. God making love to God. Now we're talking!

When we agree to become conduits for love and make ourselves available to that sacred energy, the effects on the other can be palpable and observable, even when done unilaterally and without verbal communication. One time, after making exquisite love with someone I had just met, having had no discussion about any of this, as I was walking out of his apartment, he caught himself placing his hands in the *namaste* position. He tried to cover it up by clapping a bit awkwardly, but by this time my trained hands had spontaneously responded in acknowledgment.

6) Embodying cosmic generosity. As mentioned earlier in Book 1, cosmologist Brian Swimme, author of *The Universe Is a Green Dragon*, teaches us that we are quite literally made of star stuff—the very same elements that form the stars. Therefore we, too, embody the same cosmic generosity of a supernova giving itself away so that life can happen. So what if we brought that sense of giving ourselves away to our love-making, instead of approaching it simply as a way to get our rocks off?

Surrender and the possibility for self-transcendence when it comes to sex can happen whether we are being more *yang* and assertive or *yin* and receptive. In one case we place our own needs and preferences temporarily aside, giving ourselves in service rather than in pursuit of our own pleasure. We learn to anticipate our partner's pleasure, playing their body like an exquisite and priceless Stradivarius violin. We discover what turns on our partner and drives them wild with desire. There is great satisfaction in pleasuring another. As we switch the focus from getting ourselves off to giving our partner pleasure, we think of it more as cultivating a work of art, not just a quick release. Unless we have attracted a selfish and insensitive partner, our turn will come.

Generosity begets generosity. When the energy flow changes direction and it's our turn, we relax and receive. We give ourselves permission to show our pleasure and appreciation, as we give ourselves more and more completely and allow ourselves to be taken, penetrated, if you will, by the energy of love. No matter what the plumbing or the gender identification, we can take turns and flow with the exquisite—and transgender in the ultimate sense—power of love. This is more about energetics than the mechanics of who's doing what to whom. Both as a couple and within ourselves we seek to balance our masculine and feminine energies in the yin/yang of love-making.

For some, receiving can be more of a challenge, as it entails letting go of control and opening ourselves up completely, making ourselves vulnerable. To surrender in sex requires a degree of self-awareness, self-assurance, and self-trust. We have already considered that the need for control stems from the ego and its delusions, and results in fear-driven, unhealthy expressions of power.

In terms of being able to receive, self-worth may also play a role. This is one of the issues that often comes up for healing and clearing at retreats, at the core of which is some version of "am I worthy of love?" In a more subtle sense, the fear of loss of self can be an obstacle to really letting go. There is a dissolution of self that is possible, yet it is temporary and one is always at choice. The one receiving is not forfeiting individuality. During the ego's temporary retreat, ecstasy becomes available.

What's more, in reference to loss of control, ideally it is the receiver who, through subtle signs and messages, lets the giver know new directions to explore, what is working and what is not, where the openings, limits, and boundaries lie. This presumes that the giver is invested in a shared, intimate experience, not just in getting their own needs met.

When the partners are connected and tuned in to one another, mutual surrender carries both to unspeakable heights of pleasure, expanded states of awareness, and profound and life-changing spiritual experiences. At such stratified levels, genital orgasm becomes secondary and is often unnecessary, though certainly exquisite and electrifying when it occurs.

7) Breathing into ecstasy. The importance of the breath and its connection to spirituality and spiritual practice have been emphasized elsewhere in this series. In the context of sacred sex, we can use the breath to heighten the experience, to deepen a sense of connectedness, and to slow down the pace and postpone the orgasm. For men, in particular, nothing is more effective than the intentional use of breath toward this end. Take your time and enjoy! Follow the breath deeper into ecstatic embodiment. One way to think about the word "enjoy" is embodying joy, bringing it within.

8) Expanding our sexual repertoire. We will dive deeper into this later, but in no way is the intent of this discussion about sacred sex to limit anyone's behavior. What I am suggesting, rather, is that we expand our sexual repertoire and include deeper levels of intimacy, emotions, vulnerability, and love in all aspects of our love-making. Rather

than getting stuck in a behavioral rut of getting off, try something new. Explore new ways of being and pleasuring. Take risks. Explore new behaviors. Allow a sense of lightness, fun, and exploration into sex.

9) Making it about love. As far as I am concerned, this is the most important aspect of being a good lover: to let sex be about love: sexual love, sensual love, divine love. Making love—even with a stranger—means just that. Sex becomes an expression of love. Quite literally, we are *making love*, becoming conduits for love in our relationships and sexual experiences, channeling the sacred energy of love into a world desperately in need of it.

When infused with spirit, sex becomes even hotter, more sensual, and passionately alive than ever before—lasting longer, deepening intimacy, and bringing a level of satisfaction that goes beyond the physical. If, as religions claim, God is omnipresent, then that means *everywhere*. Truly, then, we can say that God is in the blow job. Or, as a lesbian minister I know says, "God is in the musk of our lovemaking."

We have been conditioned and misled into believing that God and spirituality are sexless, staid, and boring. This is simply not true. In our most profound sexual experiences, it becomes clear: God is love; God is passion; God is life; God is sex; God is juicy; God is the Ultimate Orgasm and the "Big Bang" itself. So next time that classic "Oh God!" escapes your lips during sex, remember how appropriate that remark is, for you are indeed savoring the Divine.

Yes, becoming better lovers is a spiritual thing!

CHAPTER 29
SEXUAL ENERGY, SPIRITUAL POWER

Why is our world so "obsexed," so out of control in this area? And what is the connection to power?

Sex has been so repressed and demonized that it comes out in unhealthy expressions. In its most extreme and violent forms, the unhealthy expression of sexual and power dynamics show up as rape and sexual abuse, which are more about power than sex. It is interesting that one of the most common verbal expressions of aggression in the English language, "Screw you!"—and its more colorful alternative—allude to sex. What's more, the word *fuck* is believed to originate from an Indo-European root meaning "to strike."

In a more subtle sense, we often use sex to work out power dynamics in our relationships. Because we have not been taught about honest and congruent communicating, and because we fear conflict, we tend, to a great degree, to work out the power dynamics in relationships covertly, frequently through sex. Navigating the power dynamics in the bedroom can feel like walking through a minefield. Whoever initiates risks rejection, which can take the form of a power play: "Sorry, Honey, I have a headache," when inside we are really saying: "Screw you! Hell will freeze over before you get any tonight!" Such covert power plays are incongruent: What we say does not match what we really feel inside. They are less than powerful and unsatisfying.

Not initiating can also involve elements of power: We relinquish power due to fear of rejection, and perhaps even in subtle ways manipulate the other to begin the process, thus minimizing risk. As our sense of self becomes stronger, we learn to more easily ask for what we want without taking others' response personally.

Negotiating who's on top, who's giving or receiving, as well as the logistics of sex—when? where? how often?—can be fraught with danger. For many, the missionary position still represents an attempt to ensure the domination of man over woman, who is relegated to being merely a passive incubator or instrument for the man's pleasure.

Sometimes it all feels like walking on egg shells! Even engaging in sex for self-validation is about power in the sense that we give our power away every time we look outside ourselves for acceptance or a sense of worth.

No wonder Oscar Wilde said, "Everything in the world is about sex except sex. Sex is about power."

Sex is complex and complicated. Some people unconsciously attempt to recreate relationships with their parents through sexual dynamics—hence Freud's Oedipus and Electra complexes (which theorize about a child's unconscious desire for the opposite-sex parent and rivalry with the same-sex parent, typically occurring during early psychosexual development.)

Through fantasy and fetish others learn to work out power dynamics more intentionally. To wit, the best-selling success of "Fifty Shades of Gray" and the rising popularity of SM/BD products, clubs, and festivals.

Yes, sex is incredibly pleasurable and undoubtedly a powerful force, biochemically driven, but it is more than that. Beyond the rush of endorphins and feelings of ecstasy, it is also a vehicle for deep connection, for transcendence, for momentary freedom. We have a deep desire for all of that. We long to pop out of the prison of our minds even for a brief respite. When we open our hearts in love-making it adds another layer of emotional release and the sense of connectedness transcends the physical.

CONSCIOUS LOVE

The more in touch we are with who we are and with our soulful power, and the more that we learn to be congruent and communicate our needs, desires, and emotions in a way they can be heard, the less we need to resort to covert power plays in the bedroom. When we are established in our own power and realize that another's power does not take away from ours, we can allow sex to be a natural, stimulating, and ecstatic exchange of energy, of love—and of power.

CHAPTER 30
REDEFINING SEXY: BEYOND THE SURFACE

The truth is, most of us don't have the bone structure of an Angelina Jolie, Halle Berry, or Penélope Cruz, nor the chiseled appeal of a Ricky Martin, Ryan Gosling, or Taye Diggs. And the reality is, we're not likely to grace the cover of a fashion magazine anytime soon. Yet, how often have we met someone who, despite having all the makings of a cover model, lacked that spark—the kind of magnetism that keeps us intrigued beyond a first glance? Conversely, there are those who may not fit conventional standards of beauty, yet exude an undeniable, almost primal allure. They pull us in, ignite curiosity, and—before we know it—we're captivated, drawn in by something far beyond the surface.

So, what is this elusive quality we call sexiness? What makes someone irresistibly attractive in a way that transcends physical traits?

Sexiness is an energy—an unshakable confidence, a magnetic presence, a deep sense of self that radiates from within. It has little to do with conventional beauty and everything to do with authenticity, passion, and the way someone fully inhabits their own body and life.

It's the gleam in someone's eyes when they talk about what sets their soul on fire. It's the way they move—comfortable, unapologetic, at ease with themselves, at home in their bodies. It's the courage to be vulnerable, to take up space, to own one's desires without shame.

Sexiness is not about perfection; it's about presence. It's about being fully alive, embracing one's uniqueness, and expressing it without inhibition. It's the willingness to live boldly, love deeply, and show up to life with an open heart.

True sexiness isn't something that can be faked, bought, or forced. It's cultivated through self-awareness, self-love, and the fearless pursuit of what lights us up. And when we embody it, it's irresistible.

Sexiness is not about external features—it's about self-knowledge, self-acceptance, and the confidence that comes from doing the inner work. It's about pursuing our own unique brand of excellence, whatever that may look like. Someone who is fully engaged in their own evolution, passionately embracing life and pushing their personal limits, radiates an undeniable allure. This kind of presence—bold, unapologetic, and alive—is magnetic.

Personal excellence doesn't come with a singular definition. For one person, it might mean writing an Oscar-winning screenplay; for another, it could be perfecting the most decadent chocolate brownies on the planet. It's not about the final product—it's about the passion, the dedication, and the energy we bring to what we do. That's what makes us come alive. And that's what's sexy.

Owning our sexiness isn't just a privilege—it's our birthright. It's the natural result of knowing who we are, embracing our passions, and inhabiting our bodies with reverence and joy. No one else can give us this kind of power, and no one can take it away. It's ours to cultivate, to embody, to unleash.

Our sense of purpose makes us attractive and magnetic—which means that sex appeal is available to anyone and everyone! No excuses. No one is off the hook when it comes to sexiness! We all have access to it.

I know a woman in her late 40s, plus-sized and a single mother, who always seems to have a man; in fact, sometimes she juggles more than one at a time. Her secret? A subtle confidence that comes from knowing her worth. She doesn't wait for external validation;

she claims her own desirability. Attractiveness is a state of mind.

So if passion—in and out of the bedroom—is fueled by personal excellence and a sense of purpose, how do we ignite more of it in our lives? What is holding us back? What cobwebs need to be cleared in our belief systems? What anchors need to be lifted? What fears are keeping us playing small? What truly turns us on spiritually, or gives us a spiritual hard-on, so to speak? What brings us alive, makes time stop, puts us in "the zone?"

The way we approach life is reflected in the way we experience intimacy. Those who live with passion, who throw themselves fully into their purpose, tend to bring that same unrestrained energy into the bedroom.

It makes sense that a person's willingness to go for it, holding nothing back in relation to life purpose, would reflect on their ability to let themselves be free and passionate in the bedroom as well. That willingness to let go is connected to personal courage and a sense of adventure. Passion requires surrender—the courage to let loose, to trust, to open ourselves fully to love, to ecstasy, to life itself. We turn over our bodies as sacred vessels to be penetrated, animated, inhabited by the power and passion of love. We give ourselves to love, thereby unleashing passion.

So, ask yourself: Are you truly living your soul's purpose? Are you fully committed to your highest potential, or are you playing it safe for the illusion of security? Instead, are you willing to break free from self-imposed limitations and step into the fullness of who you were meant to be? (In Book 3 of the series, we will dive deeper into purpose and leadership.)

It is time to open our hearts, turn up the heat, and unleash our passion. When we do, we tap into power. And that's sexy. Beyond sexy. Living powerfully with purpose is not only sexy but is ultimately about survival, as demonstrated by Viktor Frankl's search for meaning in the concentration camps.

We are needed now ... living fully and passionately in every sense of the word—for our sake and for the sake of the world.

HARNESSING THE CURRENT OF SEXUAL ENERGY

Self-esteem and self-worth are intricately connected to sexual expression. Sexuality often becomes a vehicle for validating self-worth. It certainly was for me. During the dark days of adolescence, there were only two things I liked about myself: I knew I was smart and I knew I was attractive. I got enough feedback from the world to realize that people turned on to me, regardless of their gender. Flirting, whether subtly or more overtly, was often present even when there was no likelihood of sex.

During the time I spent in the ashram from age 30 to 35, I was mostly celibate. When first joining the community, one committed to a requisite year of celibacy. For someone who probably had at least an orgasm a day since age ten, and some times more than one, if you told me that I would go for a year without any kind of sexual expression, I would have laughed—or perhaps cried—in disbelief. I mean, we're talking *complete* celibacy—not even hanging out with my "five best friends!" As it turned out, however, the ashram experience was much more intense and difficult in other ways, and I found myself in such a constant state of existential shock and psychological survival, that the year actually went by pretty fast. Still, it turned out to be a highly empowering experience, one that deepened and expanded my sense of identity. During that abstinent year, beyond practicing self-control, I also began to learn to relate to people without sexual energy at play.

Sexuality, after the required year of celibacy, was acceptable—at least in theory. In practice, communal living and the rigorous demands of ashram life rendered it impossible. I could count on one hand the number of encounters I had during that period. In addition, there was an underlying sense that sexuality was something to be transcended, an appetite to be mastered. My teacher was effortlessly celibate; desire had waned in her and sexuality was no longer of interest.

As for me, I wanted to dive in fully, but now in a conscious and sacred way. Through this phase of celibacy, I began to learn to pull back my sexual energy, which, to some degree, had always governed or at least influenced my prior relationships. To be clear, there's nothing wrong or bad about sexual energy. But for me, this phase was about freeing myself. I had been controlled by sexuality, yet, for the most part, I had remained unconscious of how I was using it for validation and the subtle role it played in my interactions with others.

Years later, after having done a great deal of work on myself and with many others in this area of relationships, sexuality, and attraction, I learned to think of and use language about all this in a more nuanced way. The goal is not to suppress or make wrong the sexual energy in any way, for it is beautiful and potentially nothing less than sacred. Rather, the practice is learning how to *contain* it.

For many people, sexual energy leaks out unconsciously when we feel attracted to someone, or when we need affection, acknowledgment, or validation in some way. Suddenly, our attention and focus are all about the object of attraction. Think of it as the energetic feelers or tendrils with suction cups that we discussed earlier.

In addition to a desire to possess the other, we also send the unspoken message: "I want you because ultimately I hope you will fill a hole, a sense of emptiness in me." We then tend to obsess about that one object of desire. We must have them and no one else will do. Our power and our potential for happiness and well-being have been completely turned over to another. Talk about a power leakage!

Some seek validation in an endless stream of encounters. Do we really think any number of sexual conquests will give us the sense of self-worth we so desire? The need for self-validation has compromised many a relationship and resulted in betrayed trust, often irreparably. Unless it is healed at the source, it is insatiable and impossible to fulfill. Finding validation this way is a hopeless effort, and will only yield an endless string of empty conquests, yet another notch on the bedpost.

Sex for self-validation is ultimately not fulfilling, no matter how many conquests we make. Like the song says, we "can't get no … satisfaction!" Not really. Because of this relentless, insatiable, and unquenchable desire, we set ourselves up for the addictive elements of sexuality all too eager to kick in. When we look outside ourselves to fill an empty hole—so to speak—there is no amount of sex that can accomplish that. Only we can fulfill ourselves by addressing the issue at its core.

Containing sexual energy means we allow ourselves to feel it, while retaining an element of choice. With mindfulness and self-monitoring, we no longer automatically and unconsciously send out drippy, sticky, needy, suction cups with hooks and strings attached. We reel back in any we may have sent out and attached to others. We develop the self-discipline to hold back from reflexively projecting our sexual energy at another—making it all about them, losing our center, losing ourselves in the process. Instead we allow it to bubble up around us and envelop ourselves in it. Luxuriating in its crystal clarity and purity, we no longer feel needy but rather self-sufficient, magnetic, and attractive. We know who we are and our value as human beings does not depend on whether anyone finds us attractive. We no longer need anyone's validation, nor do we need our attraction to another reciprocated (though it sure is nice when that happens!). We also learn to feel the attraction without needing to act on it. Choice becomes part of the equation.

POWER PRACTICE

A Relationship Energy Review

Taking inventory of where your energy has been unconsciously entangled can be a powerful practice. It brings awareness to patterns, reveals where energy may be leaking, and fosters a deeper, more intentional sense of clarity and empowerment.

Step 1: Reflection and Writing

Find a quiet space with a journal or a piece of paper. Take a few deep breaths and reflect on your past and present relationships—romantic, sexual, emotional, and even unspoken infatuations or

unresolved connections.
Write down:

- Names or Initials – List anyone with whom you sense there is lingering energetic entanglement.

- Emotional Charge – Note what emotions arise when you think of each person (longing, resentment, guilt, attachment, unresolved sadness, etc.).

- Patterns & Themes – Identify any recurring themes. Do you notice a tendency to give too much? To seek validation? To become energetically entangled too quickly?

- Physical Sensations – Observe how your body responds as you think of each relationship. Do you feel tension in your chest, a knot in your stomach, a pull toward someone?

Step 2: Acknowledging Attachments and Energy Leaks

Next to each name, write:

- What you might still be holding onto. (e.g., "I still feel like I need closure," "I never fully expressed my truth," "I feel rejected and unworthy," etc.)

- How this connection may still be affecting you. (e.g., "I compare others to them," "I avoid certain emotions because of them," "I feel drained when I think about them.")

- What you are ready to release. (e.g., "The need for them to understand me," "The belief that I was unlovable," "The resentment I've held onto.")

Step 3: Setting an Intention for Reclamation

Take a moment to set a clear intention for yourself. You might say: "I am ready to release attachments that no longer serve me. I honor the experiences and lessons, but I reclaim my energy fully. I step into my power with clarity and sovereignty."

CHAPTER 31
BECOMING MAGNETIC

In the game of attraction, it is more effective to flip on the magnetism switch than to obsessively pursue or chase. By allowing the sexual energy to arise and flow, yet containing it without projecting it onto another, we become attractors, beacons, magnetic. It bears repeating: Standing free, we reel in our suction cups and gently release any that may have been attached to us. This is how we stay centered, rooted, and complete within ourselves, remaining connected to the flow of life without blocking any energies. In thus reclaiming our energy—our power—we set ourselves, and all others, free.

In the process of pulling back our suction cups, emotional stuff may be triggered—ours, the other person's, or both. Though familial attachments can be sticky, to say the least, sexual attachments are probably the most difficult to release. When we make love, we generally open to the other person's energies and make ourselves vulnerable emotionally. Fundamental issues of identity and self-worth are easily activated. The simplest acts or expressions of preference can be personalized and interpreted as rejection, plummeting us into failure or, in order to compensate, feelings that we have to make the other person or the experience wrong. Instead, we can now remain mindful of our own tendencies and reclaim our projections, without rationalizing or excusing anyone's boorish or insensitive behavior.

In addition to releasing attachments and getting clear about our purpose, here are some basic strategies for increasing our personal attractiveness and magnetism:

Know yourself. Who are you? What makes you tick? What are you passionate about? Increased self-knowledge inevitably leads to deeper levels of self-acceptance. Ironically, the freer we are and the less we need external approval, the more attractive we become.

Heal yourself. Any work we do to cultivate our own gardens and identify—and release—faulty and outmoded belief systems and outgrown and dysfunctional behavior patterns, will be useful, freeing, and empowering. The less baggage we carry, the more attractive traveling companions we become on the journey of life.

Breathing. As I have mentioned, of all healing modalities this is the most effective one I have encountered to release past trauma, catalyze healing, and let go of old baggage.

• Taking risks. Breaking out of our comfort zones and limitations can lead to personal growth, an expanded sense of self and increased self-confidence.

• Developing presence. All the above lead to a heightened sense of presence, that hard-to-define but undeniable quality that makes people attractive. I think presence is what the French mean by that certain "je ne se quois" quality.

Keeping our word. Becoming accountable and trustworthy is a simple—if not necessarily easy—practice that anyone can develop. These qualities are both empowering and attractive.

Vanishing the Victim. Refusing to buy into the victim role and assuming responsibility for our lives are likewise attractive and liberating qualities.

CHAPTER 32
NEW HORIZONS IN SEXUALITY

Old cultural taboos and outdated collective thought forms about sexuality began to be questioned and to quickly unravel during the sexual revolution of the '60s and '70s, together with and as an expression of the women's liberation movement. The pill accelerated the process when it was introduced in the '60s, helping to disentangle sex from its reproductive function. For many, the ensuing dissolution of rules and an "anything goes" permissiveness resulted in multiple sexual partners.

With the onset of AIDS in the 80s, an adjustment—a reality check—was forced upon this time of sexual awakening. The sex/death connection so undeniable to women throughout history became obvious to us all, regardless of our HIV status. Had the pendulum perhaps swung too far?

My thoughts here are not about morality. I will share my perceptions about that in the next section. However, for me the cutting edge of sex is not horizontal—in numbers. How many more partners will it take for us to realize that purely sexual experiences are not always fulfilling, and sometimes leave us feeling emptier than before? Rather, the cutting edge is vertical: how high and how deep can we take the experience of making love? That's exciting! That's the real—and limitless—frontier.

When we choose freedom from society's rules and conditioning, we get to make up our own rules. What, then, might those be? Or does anything go, anytime, anywhere? How does morality figure in this exploration of the sexual wilderness?

CHAPTER 33
OUTRAGEOUS MORALITY

What right does a gay man who espouses no specific religion have to comment on moral values? That was the first thing that occurred to me when the idea came through to tackle this question. Some years ago, I served as a consultant for the National LGBTQ Force, the oldest lesbian, gay, bisexual, and transgender rights national organization, coordinating a project on issues of religion, faith-based organizing, spirituality, and moral values. At the time, they had received a grant from a foundation to explore specifically the issue of morality.

As my attention tuned in to this matter, I read several books issued by the then-burgeoning "Religious Left," including Rabbi Michael Lerner's *The Left Hand of God*, Rev. Jim Wallis's *God's Politics* and former President Jimmy Carter's *Our Endangered Values*—these last two Southern Baptists. Spiritual luminaries like the Dalai Lama (*Ethics for the New Millennium*) and retired Episcopal Bishop John Shelby Spong (*Sins of Scripture*) also released books on this subject. With a slightly more moderate perspective, former Republican Senator and Episcopal priest John Danforth (*Faith and Politics*) and David Callahan (*The Moral Center*) added their voice to the choir—all striving to expand the conversation about moral values and to reclaim from the Religious Right the moral high ground for a more universal and inclusive perspective.

For the past few decades, a small but powerful minority with a very specific, narrow, and inflexible view of what is right and wrong has dominated the conversation about morality in our "public square." Combined with a religiously fueled mandate to impose their views on the rest of us—with the conviction of their beliefs and the best of intentions in mind, I am sure—this group has persuasively penetrated the government from local school boards to the White House, the U.S. Supreme Court, and the Pentagon. As a result, for many people today, the word "morality" connotes two things predominantly: abortion and homosexuality.

For many people, how I express my love and my sexuality is cause enough to condemn me to eternal damnation. Some will no doubt be outraged by this book. Of significance is the fact that many, if not most, religious institutions today are experiencing at least internal conflict while some even face the possibility of schism over the issue of LGBTQ inclusion. The irony of this state of affairs, however, is that long ago, before patriarchal cultures and religions became predominant, people we today refer to as LGBT, or queer, were not only spiritually inclined, but were often respected for their moral leadership and for the spiritual roles they fulfilled. I have covered this premise extensively in *Coming Out Spiritually*.

So what does this gay man have to say about morality? Quite a bit, as it turns out. To do so, I draw upon a rich spiritual heritage, which many of my LGBTQ sisters and brothers are also actively reclaiming. I also draw upon my own personal experience, including a strong Catholic upbringing, a brief flirtation with the Jesuits at an earlier age, and five years in an Eastern-based ashram. Most importantly, I claim that right as a human being living on this most exquisite and imperiled Planet Earth, for which—including all its inhabitants—I care more deeply that I can express.

What I find outrageously immoral is that the conversation about moral values has been co-opted to establish power and dominance over others, to exploit and threaten the destruction of the environment, to enslave people in myriad ways, to diminish women and children, to justify wars and the killing and maiming of countless humans under false pretenses and in the name of God.

What I find outrageously immoral is the way we treat each other. In my experience and view of life, the sacred, by whichever name or form we relate to it, is found everywhere, and certainly within all living creatures. How dare we abuse or mistreat any being?

What I find outrageously immoral is the total lack of respect with which we treat our bodies—through addiction of all kinds, through the chemicals in our food, the air we breathe, and the water we drink. We disrespect our bodies by letting these miracles of efficiency, subtlety, complexity, and raw beauty go soft and flaccid, unhealthy and underused.

What I find outrageously immoral is how we fail to recognize the magnificence inherent in every human each time we rape or steal from or neglect or exclude or look down on or discriminate against another simply because of their skin pigmentation, where they were born, what they believe, what's between their legs and what they do with that.

What I find outrageously immoral is multinational corporations pillaging virgin rain forests, and a consumer culture that foments greed and cut-throat competition with utter disregard for the environment and for the effect such actions and stances have on our very survival.

What I find outrageously immoral is the condition in which we are leaving this planet for generations to come.

What I find outrageously immoral is the misuse of technology to promote violence and to create unimaginably barbaric and increasingly devastating weapons of mass destruction. And the injudicious, greed-driven use of complex chemicals that are ravaging our disease-ridden bodies and planet.

What I find outrageously immoral is the ever-growing gap between rich and poor — and the staggering reality that, as of 2024, 1.93 billion people struggle to survive on less than $3.65 a day.[10] What I find outrageously immoral is that executive compensation continues to rise to the stratosphere as corporations squeeze more and more out the benefits and lifetime savings of their employees.

What I find outrageously immoral is ego-driven, power-addicted political leaders who neglect the need of the people they were elected to serve. What I find outrageously immoral is the lies we are continually told by our leaders.

What I find outrageously immoral is that corporations have been deemed to be people by the U.S. Supreme Court and that our elections are now unduly influenced by multibillionaires.

What I find outrageously immoral is religious leaders hypocritically demonizing LGBTQ people while secretly and deceitfully engaging in extramarital relations and other ethical lapses. What I find outrageously immoral is bishops covering up the abuses of pederast priests in order to protect the dwindling reputation and status of their church, while scapegoating gay priests and seminarians for those wrongs.

What I find outrageously immoral is the suffering and inner conflict experienced by untold millions of people throughout history—of every sexual persuasion—because of mistaken, mistranslated, and misinterpreted moral teachings, teachings selectively earmarked and taken out of their cultural and historical context.

And what I most find outrageously immoral is when religions have turned God into a petty, punitive, micromanaging, domineering, lifeless, judgmental, insipid, pleasure-hating busybody and control-freak. What a small, petty God we have created in our very own image! *That* is morally outrageous. *That* is the abomination, not whom I love or how I express my passion.

CHAPTER 34
STAGES OF MORALITY: EVOLVING BEYOND RIGHT AND WRONG

All right, now that that litany is out of my system, for those of us who are not going to base our moral choices on texts that are thousands of years old and that have been edited, redacted, mistranslated, misinterpreted and taken out of context, or those of us who hesitate to give power over our personal lives to any institution or another human being, how do we navigate the question of what is right and wrong for ourselves, particularly in this fiery and complicated area of human sexuality?

I realize there are complex and nuanced discussions to be had about morality. Entire college philosophy courses are taught and huge texts have been written on the subject. The reality is, however, that most people are never going to tackle one of those texts, which can be dense, hard to understand, and less than stimulating reading. Furthermore, this whole question of morality is inextricably connected to the realm of religion, which, for many, has forfeited its moral high ground due to hypocrisy, inflexibility, and inconsistency.

So here is my simple (some might say simplistic) contribution to help us navigate the question of what is right and wrong, particularly in the sexual arena.

As I see it, there are four basic stages of moral development:

1) Punishment
2) Karma
3) The Golden Rule
4) Namaste

Clearly, our perceptions of and relationship to morality evolve. At some point in our lives—and also as a species—we needed external motivation, that is, the fear of punishment (whether being sent to bed, jail, or hell, or the threat of divorce) to keep our behavior in line and a semblance of order in society. Regrettably, this is still the case—and perhaps a necessary evil—for far too many of us.

As we continue to grow and evolve, whether because we internalize social rules or, as scientific evidence indicates, we are hard wired for compassion and cooperation, we increasingly assume responsibility for our own actions and no longer need to be told what's right or wrong. Incidentally, this is one way morality relates to power. We reclaim our personal power by shifting the focus of responsibility and accountability within, rather than depending on external sources.

The second stage, and an important guiding principle for behavior, is the law of karma: What goes around comes around. Though more evolved a motivator than fear of punishment, at its most basic interpretation the law of karma is still somewhat punitive and based on cosmic retribution: I won't harm you because those actions will come back and hurt me.

A more evolved level in moral development is Stage 3, the Golden Rule. Also called the Ethic of Reciprocity, a version of it is found in almost every religion.[11] It is certainly true that if we treated others the way we want to be treated, the world would be a very different place. We might say that another version of this is "Love Your Neighbor as Yourself."

CONSCIOUS LOVE

The ultimate stage of moral development comes as a result of the realization that we share a common humanity. We can think of this level as the Namaste Way. If I believe that the sacred resides both in you and me, how can I steal from you, lie to you, rape you, kill you, cheat on you, or invade and exploit your country? Perhaps this coincides with Jesus' more challenging "Love your enemy" directive, which also requires seeing the sacred, or at least the best, in everyone, whether or not we like, look like, or agree with them. Incidentally, the concept that the Divine resides inside each of us is not exclusive to Hinduism and is, in fact, fairly universal.

CHAPTER 35
SEXUAL ETHICS: (SO ... WHO AND WHAT CAN WE DO?)

Our commitment is to maintaining our own integrity, meaning wholeness and congruence, in all areas of our lives. In terms of sexual ethics, our relationships are congruent with who we are.

So what are the rules? Who and what can we do?

In my view, as long as no one is getting harmed, the decision of whether expressions of love and sexual passion between two (or more, for that matter) consenting adults are appropriate or moral is best left to the individuals involved. Who am I to decide what's right or wrong for anyone else? Figuring that out for myself is challenging enough!

My rules—the ones I use to guide my own behavior—are simple, though their interpretation and implementation may not be easy.

DO NO HARM

What are the implications of this? For me, Do No Harm means, for example, that I do not—knowingly—sleep with people who are in relationship with or married to someone else, unless they have an agreement or understanding about that. And boy, has honoring this been challenging a number of times! However, to the best of my ability, I choose not to be part of potentially causing harm to another.

Another situation with which many of us struggle is: "Do I stay in a relationship with a person I enjoy and with whom I feel comfortable but who is ultimately not what I am looking for?" My "Do No Harm" take on this is that long as we are honest and upfront about how we hold the relationship (we're fuck buddies, or friends with benefits) and not mislead others, this is OK. However, the Do No Harm directive also includes harm to self. So a deeper question may be: "Am I short-selling myself—and the other person—for the mutual convenience and comfort of a steady lay?"

Neither of these questions is easy to discern or act upon. When things are not clear, I revert to my guidance and intuition and listen to the deeper messages from my heart and my gut. Sometimes I consult a trusted advisor.

Other variations to ponder in this arena of No Harm to Self include:

- "Am I placing myself in a situation that is somehow not good or healthy for me?"

- "Do I continue to pursue the hot one who is great in the sack but not available emotionally?"

To help navigate such issues, I ask myself the following questions that can help in getting clear about what works and does not work for me (*Note: The first two were adapted from a lecture given years ago by my friend Bob Barzan):

1) How do I feel afterwards?

2) Will (or did) the experience, does the relationship—or the behavior—make me a better, more loving, open and compassionate person? Or is it leading to separation, rather than communication, contraction rather than expansion?

3) Is love present? One of my guidelines is that love has to be present. Even with someone I just met, I consciously invoke the energy of love before and during the experience.

4) Is it a match?

My last standard is: "Is it congruent with who I am? Does it match my energy?" Too often we have sold out on our standards for immediate gratification, to avoid being alone, or for the elusive promise of love. In a sense, this conversation is not even about morality, but rather, about raising our personal standards and discovering what is a match, congruent and appropriate for us now. For me, that means there has to be a spiritual connection, even if it is not labeled that. It does not mean that we have to sit in meditation, gaze deeply into each other's eyes, and chant OM before making love, but a connection at the heart level has to be present, even with someone I just met. I've learned that when that is missing, I walk away from the experience feeling empty.

CHAPTER 36
RETHINKING CELIBACY AND MONOGAMY

When I first met my former teacher at a weekend intensive over 35 years ago, I rushed to the front of the room before a break, hoping to catch her before she stepped out. I had one pressing question I needed to ask her: "Do I have to give up sex to become enlightened?" She laughed.

If sex is in fact sacred, why do several spiritual traditions recommend celibacy? Is sexuality a trap of the flesh?

At 19, falling deeply in love forced me to confront a choice—between my true self and the religious beliefs I had inherited. To put things in perspective, in Catholic doctrine, even masturbation is considered a mortal sin—let alone the unmentionable one that weighed heavily on my mind. That moment sparked a long journey of deconstructing old conditioning and rebuilding a belief system that felt authentic. In my twenties, I began questioning whether monogamy was truly a universal default. While fidelity came naturally to me, I repeatedly found myself with partners who struggled with it. Was this just a matter of character, or were some people simply wired differently?

Scientific studies on genetic influences in animals suggested that biology might play a role. Monogamy has evolved independently in various animal species, suggesting that it offers evolutionary advantages. These advantages often relate to increased offspring survival, particularly when both parents are needed to provide care.

Humans also have a very long childhood development, which increases the likelihood that collaborative parental care is a helpful evolutionary trait. However, while genetics may predispose individuals toward monogamy or non-monogamy, human relationships are shaped by a complex interplay of biology, psychology, culture, and personal choice. Unlike animals, humans can consciously decide how they structure their relationships, making monogamy—or any relationship style—a choice rather than a strictly hardwired trait.

Far more damaging is what tends to happen most often: the partners commit to monogamy and then cheat and lie about it, until they end up getting caught. Lying is the slow death of relationships. It takes up so much psychic space to maintain a lie and try not to get caught, and a lie, no matter how small, will eat up space otherwise available for communication, for simply being with each other. As we saw earlier, that is what suffocates relationships.

A mentor once introduced me to the concept of high vs. low monogamy. Low monogamy is driven by fear—fear of consequences, social judgment, or religious guilt. High monogamy, on the other hand, is a conscious choice, made with full awareness and integrity. The same applies to open relationships. The question isn't whether one model is better than the other, but whether the choice is made from truth, rather than fear or conditioning.

I have learned that there are many models of relationship, that the issues are complex and that to get beneath the social conditioning is a challenging yet worthwhile endeavor. As far as I am concerned, as Socrates said, the unexamined life is not worth living.

HOW DO SPIRITUAL TRADITIONS VIEW CELIBACY?

It was not until the Council of Elvira around 306 CE that celibacy was mandated for Catholic clergy. According to many scholars, however, the impetus for this was inheritance rights: the Church sought to ensure that the wealth of its leaders stayed with the church.

In Judaism and Islam, celibacy is not considered a spiritual ideal. Generally, Buddhism only recommends celibacy for those on the monastic path. Even after he settled on the Middle Path after diving deep into asceticism, the Buddha still considered celibacy as an ideal. Yet, according to the Dalai Lama, celibacy is not necessary to attain enlightenment. [12]

Drawing from the Hindu tradition, Ram Dass delineates two possible approaches to sexuality, both of which he considers valid. The first, *brahmacharya,* involves sexual continence for the purpose of transmuting and rechanneling the sexual energies from the second chakra up the spine into higher energy centers. The intention is to apply the sexual energies toward the process of enlightenment. By effectively converting these energies, the practitioner is able to avoid sexual frustration by experiencing high meditative and even blissful states.

The second, sexual tantra, involves the arousal of sexual energies but intentionally redirecting them into spiritual realms. Both partners consciously approach the sexual experience for the intention of purification and, ultimately, sacred union.

Indigenous traditions generally do not impose celibacy as a spiritual requirement. Instead, they often view sexuality as a sacred and natural aspect of life, deeply connected to the cycles of nature, fertility, and spiritual energy. Many Indigenous cultures incorporate rites of passage, vision quests, or periods of abstinence for specific ceremonial or shamanic purposes, but this is typically temporary and intention-driven rather than a lifelong mandate. Sexuality is often seen as a powerful force that, when honored with respect and responsibility, can be a source of vitality, connection, and even spiritual awakening.

When we step outside of the realms of social rules and conditioning and leave behind concepts of a punitive deity, the journey to freedom becomes one of heroic exploration, self-discovery, and fulfillment. Our morality becomes more nuanced and mature, internally driven. We give ourselves the gift of exploring the limitless boundaries of spirituality and sexuality. And we are always at choice. May your journey be graceful and fun!

THE SANCTUARY OF CONSCIOUS LOVE

Love, at its core, is both a journey and a sanctuary—a sacred space we create within ourselves and with others. When we approach love consciously, we shift from seeking validation to offering presence, from fearing loss to embracing connection, and from repeating old wounds to forging new possibilities. We step into love not as passive recipients but as active co-creators, cultivating relationships that nourish the soul and inspire our highest potential.

This path is not always easy. It requires courage, honesty, and a willingness to examine the hidden beliefs and patterns that shape our relational experiences. It calls us to take responsibility for our part in the dance of love, to recognize the barriers we place between ourselves and intimacy, and to release the outdated stories that keep us stuck in cycles of pain or longing. Conscious love demands that we show up fully—raw, vulnerable, and open-hearted. It is the stuff of heroes.

Yet, when we do this work, we begin to taste the deep joy and freedom that love in its highest form offers. Love ceases to be a battlefield or a transaction and becomes a sanctuary—a place where we are truly seen, honored, and cherished for who we are.

In this sanctuary, there is no need for masks or pretense. There is only truth, devotion, and a shared commitment to growth.

This is the invitation of Conscious Love: to create relationships that are not built on illusion or expectation but on the solid foundation of authenticity, mutual respect, and soulful connection. To recognize that love is not something we find but something we become. To trust that when we love from a place of wholeness, we naturally attract relationships that reflect our deepest truth.

CONSCIOUS LOVE

And so, as we step forward from this exploration, may we do so with open hearts and steady hands. May we become the love we seek, knowing that in doing so, we create a world where love is not only possible—it is inevitable.

PART VI

EMBODYING CONSCIOUS LOVE

CHAPTER 37
SUCCESSFUL RELATIONSHIPS

Love and sexuality are deeply intertwined—both are portals to connection, intimacy, and transformation. As we explored in Part 5, conscious sexuality is not just about physical pleasure; it is about presence, reverence, and the merging of body, heart, and soul. When approached with awareness, it becomes a powerful expression of love itself—a sacred dance between the human and the divine.

And yet, sexuality is just one facet of the greater whole. True, lasting love requires more than chemistry and passion; it calls for intention, commitment, and an ever-deepening understanding of ourselves and our partners.

As we arrive at the final chapters of this journey, we bring all the pieces together—the insights, the practices, the breakthroughs—and distill them into the essential elements of conscious, thriving relationships. In this final section, we reflect on what it truly means to love, to be loved, and to create relationships that uplift, heal, and inspire.

10 ELEMENTS OF SUCCESSFUL RELATIONSHIPS

Navigating and maintaining a conscious relationship is no small feat. It requires self-awareness, emotional maturity, and a willingness to grow—both individually and together. Unlike fairy-tale notions of love, conscious relationships demand effort, patience, and the courage to face our own fears and insecurities. They challenge us to evolve, to communicate with honesty, and to practice deep compassion. At times, the journey can feel overwhelming, but when approached with intention, relationships become one of life's greatest opportunities for healing and transformation.

While no formula guarantees success, certain foundational elements can greatly enhance the depth, resilience, and fulfillment of a conscious partnership. Think of the following list as a recap of our work together so far.

1) Nurturing a strong sense of self: The stronger our inner foundation, the less likely we are to lose ourselves in a relationship. This requires deep self-awareness. It means going within. To the extent that we look to another for validation, acceptance, or completion, we are setting ourselves up for disappointment.

2) Understanding love vs. being "in love": Remember, that intoxicating, butterflies-in-the-stomach feeling is not love—it's a fleeting state, a trick of nature designed for species survival. Love is not just an emotion; it is a conscious choice, an ongoing act of devotion, presence, and care.

3) Mastering the ego: The ego thrives on projection—blaming others for what is unhealed within us. True relationship work involves turning the mirror around, developing emotional intelligence, and recognizing when our wounds are distorting our perceptions.

4) Practicing patience and perseverance: Relationships go through cycles, and difficult moments are inevitable. The key is staying committed through the discomfort, trusting that "this too shall pass" and that growth often comes through the fire of transformation.

CONSCIOUS LOVE

And then, the 6 Cs:

5) Showing compassion: From the Latin *compati*, meaning "to suffer with," true compassion means stepping into another's shoes while maintaining self-respect. It also leads to forgiveness—letting go of the need to be "right" and allowing space for both people to be imperfectly human.

6) Honoring commitment: Not just to the relationship itself, but to mutual growth, even if the shape of the relationship evolves. Commitment also means keeping the heart open, even in conflict. The heart cannot be closed selectively. Love cannot be shut off to just some—it either flows or it doesn't.

7) Cultivating the garden: Relationships, like gardens, require care. We must weed out resentments, nurture connection, and create space for open, honest, and authentic communication. Neglect leads to overgrowth—unspoken tensions, unmet needs, and eventual disconnection. Commit to doing the hard work of relationships, to weeding the garden. Otherwise there will be no space for honest, authentic, real communication.

8) Developing communication and radical honesty: Every lie, omission, or avoidance partitions off a part of ourselves from the relationship. Radical honesty doesn't mean being unkind; it means showing up fully and speaking truth with love. We can face the truth, no matter how difficult—but it's the lies that break us.

9) Finding compromise and balance: No one "wins" in a power struggle without the relationship losing. Healthy partnerships require learning the art of fair negotiation, finding middle ground, and understanding that compromise does not mean self-betrayal.

10) Creating community: We are not meant to navigate relationships alone. Seek support, whether through trusted friends, mentors, or spiritual guidance. Invite the sacred into your relationship—whether through shared rituals, mindfulness, or simply holding the partnership as a vessel for mutual evolution.

At its highest, relationship is not just about companionship—it is a path of growth, healing, and awakening.

> "WE ARE BORN IN RELATIONSHIP, WE ARE WOUNDED IN RELATIONSHIP, AND WE ARE HEALED IN RELATIONSHIP."
> — HARVILLE HENDRIX

CHAPTER 38
CHOOSE LOVE

Amo Ergo Sum: The Power of Love

Soulful Power is ultimately about love. The call to power is a call to love, to radical love. What does that mean? Of course, we are not talking about a saccharine, Hallmark, milquetoast kind of love, but the "grab the elephant by the balls" kind of love Hafiz described in *A Barroom View of Love*. The kind of love that rocks the world: the heroic act of keeping our hearts open no matter what.

Love is not wimpy or airy-fairy. Love is fierce. Love is power. Love transcends all, including time and space.

Jimi Hendrix said that, "When the power of love conquers the love of power then the world will know peace." Anodea Judith expands this concept and applies it to the evolutionary process of humanity: We are currently experiencing a leap in evolution from the "love of power" (based in the third chakra, the center of power) to the "power of love" (based in the fourth chakra, the heart center.)[13]

> WE ARE ENTERING THE AGE OF THE HEART. WHAT IS NOW CALLED FOR IS A NEW MOTTO FOR THIS NEW ERA IN WHICH "AMO ERGO SUM" REPLACES DESCARTES' "COGITO ERGO SUM."
> I AM . . . NOT BECAUSE I THINK, BUT BECAUSE I LOVE.

I don't believe in a punitive God or a Last Judgment. But if there were such a thing, and I were hired to produce that event,

I would want to know how much—not whom—did you love.

We have no more time for playing it safe. Clearly, that does not mean being stupid or careless, setting ourselves up for abuse, failure, or rejection. Or becoming doormats. It means taking charge, taking our lives into our hands.

This is not likely to happen on the couch watching TV or working 60-hour weeks. We must be willing to dive fully into our lives and take risks. So what if we get hurt again? We'll get over it and grow from it and emerge stronger and wiser. For every 100 times we have fallen, we have gotten up 101. We rise again, opening our hearts, no matter what.

Keeping the heart open, doing the hard work of loving, is not a path for the faint of heart. In fact, it is the stuff of heroes. As we saw in Book 1, "courage" comes from the French *cour* for heart. The heart cannot be closed selectively. It's like a shutter of a camera. We either open it or we don't. Whenever we close it to any one person who hurt us, or to a group of people who look, think, believe, pray, or love differently than we do, we are shutting off part of our heart, period.

This is the profound wisdom behind Jesus's radical teachings to "love your enemy." Literally, not metaphorically, we keep our hearts, our heart centers, our energy centers, open to everyone, no matter what.

We choose love. We let it be about love.

Our work is becoming hollow reeds for the cosmic force of love to flow through us. In her song "Trust Love," Rikki Byers reminds us that we are "givers and receivers of love." How simple is that? Our jobs are therefore laid out for us. How much love can we give and how much can we receive? Ultimately, that is our purpose!

We are infinite vessels of love. Our task is to keep the channels clear, removing any obstacles where love might get stuck. Like the hollow reeds the Buddhists speak of, we become the conduits through which love flows freely.

We are Love's Keepers—not in a hoarding sense, of course, but as stewards. We tend to its needs. We become fluid. We become permeable to the substance of love, let it flow through us. We can

CONSCIOUS LOVE

never trap it or contain it, but we can be vessels for it. We keep ourselves clear and it will find us worthy. All we have to do is say "Yes" to love's call.

What would Love do?

LOVE IS A SACRED RESERVE OF ENERGY; IT IS LIKE THE BLOOD OF SPIRITUAL EVOLUTION.
—TEILHARD DE CHARDIN

CHAPTER 39
EMBODYING CONSCIOUS LOVE IN EVERYDAY LIFE

We have journeyed together through the depths of conscious relationships—unearthing what it means to love with awareness, courage, and authenticity. Along the way, we have confronted our internal barriers to love, shedding the outdated conditioning that once held us back. We have redefined love itself, not as a fleeting emotion, but as a profound and sacred force—one that invites us into deeper connection with ourselves, with others, and with the divine.

Through this exploration, we have expanded our emotional intelligence, refining our ability to navigate relationships with clarity, empathy, and integrity. We have broadened our communication skills, learning to express our needs and desires with honesty, while also creating space for the truths of those we love. We have dared to explore sexuality—not as a taboo, but as a sacred, powerful, transformative force. We have questioned morality, not through the lens of dogma or social conditioning, but by anchoring ourselves in conscious choice and personal truth.

And now, here we are.

So what will you do with all of this?

Knowledge is powerful, but only when applied. Conscious love is not an abstract concept to be admired from a distance—it is an active, living practice. It is an ongoing journey of showing up, of choosing vulnerability over self-protection, of remaining open even when fear tempts you to close.

Will you take this wisdom and integrate it into your daily life? Will you commit to loving more fully, communicating more honestly, and embracing intimacy—both emotional and physical—with greater presence? Will you allow love to become not just something you seek, but something you embody?

This is your invitation. To live and love consciously. To remove the final barriers that stand between you and the love you truly desire. To step into the unknown with trust, knowing that real love is not something to be controlled or possessed—it is something to be experienced, moment by moment, with a heart wide open.

The path of conscious love is not always easy. It requires courage, self-awareness, and an unwavering commitment to truth. But it is worth every moment of the journey.

What's next for you? That is yours to decide.

May you walk forward with an open heart, with curiosity and reverence, and with the deep knowing that love—true, conscious love—is not something you must earn. It is who you are.

ENDNOTES

1. American Heart Association. (2024). *Is broken heart syndrome real?* Retrieved from https://www.heart.org/en/health-topics/cardiomyopathy/what-is-cardiomyopathy-in-adults/is-broken-heart-syndrome-real
2. Siegel, J. K., Kung, S. Y., Wroblewski, K. E., Kern, D. W., McClintock, M. K., & Pinto, J. M. (2021). Olfaction is associated with sexual motivation and satisfaction in older men and women. *The Journal of Sexual Medicine*, 18(2), 295. https://doi.org/10.1016/j.jsxm.2020.12.002
3. Divorce.com. (2024). *Divorce Rates in the World: Divorce Rates by County*. Retrieved from https://divorce.com/blog/divorce-rates-in-the-world/
4. Taibbi, Robert. (2024). *5 Risks for People Marrying a Second or Third Time*. Retrieved from https://www.psychologytoday.com/us/blog/fixing-families/202401/5-dangers-and-opportunities-for-second-and-third-marriages
5. Kroll, Michele M. (2022). *Prolonged Social Isolation and Loneliness are Equivalent to Smoking 15 Cigarettes A Day*. Retrieved from https://extension.unh.edu/blog/2022/05/prolonged-social-isolation-loneliness-are-equivalent-smoking-15-cigarettes-day
6. Sbarra, David. (2016). Divorce and Health: Current Trends and Future Directions. *PMC National Institutes of Health*. Retrieved from https://pmc.ncbi.nlm.nih.gov/articles/PMC4397145

7. Mineo, Liz. (2017, April 11). *Good genes are nice, but joy is better.* Harvard Gazette. Retrieved from https://news.harvard.edu/gazette/story/2017/04/over-nearly-80-years-harvard-study-has-been-showing-how-to-live-a-healthy-and-happy-life/

8. Hafiz. (1999). *The Gift: Poems by Hafiz, the Great Sufi Master.* (D. Ladinsky, Trans.). Penguin Compass.

9. Straits Research. (2025, February 20). *Perfume Market Size to Surpass USD 88.35 Billion by 2033.* GlobeNewswire. Retrieved from https://www.globenewswire.com/news-release/2025/02/20/3029472/0/en/Perfume-Market-Size-to-Surpass-USD-88-35-Billion-by-2033-Straits-Research.html

10. World Bank. (2025). *Poverty and Inequality Platform* [Data set]. Retrieved from https://pip.worldbank.org/home

11. Ontario Consultants on Religious Tolerance. *religioustolerance.org*. Formerly retrieved from http://www.religioustolerance.org/reciproc.htm [Accessed February 11, 2025 (site inactive)].

12. Editor VOPUS. *Celibacy and Tantric Buddhism.* Retrieved from http://www.vopus.org/en/gnosis/alchemy/celibacy-and-tantric-buddhism.html

13. Judith, Anodea. *The Global Heart Awakens: Humanity's Rite of Passage from the Love of Power to the Power of Love* (Carlsbad, CA: Shift Books, 2013).

ABOUT THE AUTHOR

With over 30 years of experience as a spiritual teacher and transformation coach, Christian de la Huerta helps clients break through self-doubt and emotional blocks to create relationships rooted in authenticity, depth, and conscious connection. An award-winning author, TEDx speaker, and leader in the breathwork community, Christian guides individuals on a journey of personal empowerment, purpose, and profound transformation.

His latest book, *Conscious Love: Transforming Our Relationship to Relationships*, offers a groundbreaking approach to love—challenging old paradigms and providing practical tools to cultivate deeper, more intentional relationships. His previous book, *Awakening the Soul of Power*, was praised by music icon Gloria Estefan as "a balm for the soul of anyone searching for truth and answers to life's difficult questions" and has earned multiple prestigious awards, including the Nautilus Book Award, the Global Book Award, the Book Excellence Award, and the Nonfiction Book Award.

Through his writing, retreats, and coaching, Christian empowers people to transform their relationships—not just with others, but with themselves—so they can step fully into their power and live with greater purpose and love.

INDEX

A
acceptance 21, 22, 27, 35, 43, 44, 45, 68, 95, 149, 204, 208, 216, 238
accountability 61, 64, 86, 87, 88, 89, 145, 224
Amo Ergo Sum 61, 64, 86, 87, 88, 89, 145, 224
anger 28, 49, 72, 77, 92, 94, 95, 97, 102, 105, 106, 107, 109, 113, 118, 154
art of loving 35, 51
ashram 50, 210, 220
attachment 179, 183, 186, 213
attraction 22, 42, 173, 185, 211, 212, 215
authenticity 33, 61, 64, 100, 122, 143, 147, 160, 162, 164, 207, 234, 245, 249

B
being right 36, 55, 56, 57, 120, 170
beliefs 25, 31, 35, 39, 41, 45, 95, 108, 109, 123, 130, 131, 133, 134, 135, 136, 137, 139, 140, 142, 143, 145, 146, 148, 153, 185, 193, 197, 220, 231, 234
blame 26, 33, 55, 56, 61, 64, 65, 92, 117, 118, 165, 169
blindspots 58, 59, 135
"Boss from Hell" story 61
boundaries 22, 28, 34, 51, 52, 57, 60, 95, 105, 109, 113, 115, 120, 142, 148, 163, 165, 168, 185, 186, 191, 201, 233
brahmacharya 233
breathwork 70, 71, 72, 73, 83, 110, 111, 120, 136, 137, 175, 176, 181, 249
Broken Heart Syndrome 21

C
celibacy 210, 231, 232, 233, 248
change 30, 60, 61, 67, 71, 72, 79, 92, 100, 111, 124, 143, 163, 165, 167, 168, 171, 172, 183, 198
Clearing the Space 156
comfort zone 52, 108
commitment 25, 29, 30, 39, 40, 41, 60, 64, 76, 137, 139, 159, 162, 171, 175, 177, 178, 180, 181, 227, 234, 237, 239, 246
communication 25, 28, 29, 33, 36, 77, 98, 99, 100, 110, 115, 116, 117, 118, 119, 120, 121, 122, 123, 124, 125, 146, 154, 155, 156, 184, 199, 228, 232, 239, 245
   conscious communication 116, 117, 119, 121, 122, 123, 125
   pitfalls 116
   styles 185
conditioning 25, 44, 70, 93, 130, 160, 197, 217, 231, 232, 233, 245
connection 26, 28, 32, 39, 43, 44, 53, 56, 57, 61, 64, 71-80, 82-

84, 86, 88, 98, 100, 103, 108, 115-125, 129, 137, 140, 141, 142, 147, 149, 156, 157, 160, 161, 163, 164, 170, 174, 177, 183, 185, 191, 201, 203, 204, 213, 217, 229, 233, 234, 237, 239, 245, 249, 267
conscious 23, 25, 26, 28, 31, 32, 33, 34, 35, 36, 41, 43, 44, 46, 47, 56, 67, 75, 81, 85, 87, 88, 98, 101, 105, 106, 112, 115-117, 119, 120-125, 130, 133, 143, 145-147, 153-155, 168-170, 173, 176, 178, 179, 181, 183, 184, 190, 191, 210, 232, 234, 237, 238, 245, 246, 249, 267
conscious relationships 23, 25, 26, 28, 31, 33, 34, 35, 36, 46, 47, 67, 75, 85, 87, 133, 146, 154, 155, 237, 245
control 22, 27, 33, 45, 55, 61, 63, 79, 92, 93, 95-98, 105, 107, 112, 122, 142, 144, 160, 161, 163, 164, 165, 168, 174, 180, 181, 189, 193, 200, 201, 203, 210, 222
co-op garden 77, 153, 154
core 23, 59, 70, 111, 133, 134, 135, 136, 139, 140, 143, 177, 200, 212, 234
courage 44, 60, 61, 64, 76, 91, 94, 98-100, 119, 122, 140, 143, 146, 147, 162, 163, 169, 208, 209, 234, 237, 242, 245, 246

D

Dalai Lama 49, 219, 233
dependence xiii
Descartes 241
desire 40, 45, 69, 102, 105, 134, 140, 161, 168, 179, 180, 183, 184, 200, 204, 210- 212, 246
Dhyan, Maia 70, 106, 154

divorce 31, 32, 55, 143, 145, 176, 224, 247

E

ecstasy
 meaning of 22
ego, the
 boundaries 22, 51, 148, 191
Emotional Intelligence (EQ) 106
Emotional Seesaw 106
emotions
 categories of 22, 26, 27, 28, 33, 36, 48, 65, 72, 91, 92, 93, 94, 95, 96, 97, 98, 99, 100, 101, 105, 106, 109-116, 118, 121, 124, 145, 153, 174, 181, 201, 205, 213
 grid 106
 lexicon 101
 list of 41, 106, 148, 184
 mastery of 112
 triggers 27, 34, 97, 101, 107, 109, 117, 120, 124
empowerment 61, 63, 71, 87, 98, 100, 143, 159, 160-163, 165, 168, 212, 249
Ethic of Reciprocity 224
expectations 25, 26, 27, 29, 35, 39, 41, 46, 55, 62, 94, 102, 103, 109, 139, 148, 162, 183

F

falling in love 35, 51, 52, 135
fear 27, 30, 40, 41, 43, 62, 92, 94, 95, 96, 99, 110, 118, 121, 123, 136, 139, 140-143, 147, 149, 155, 156, 157, 162, 163, 167, 168, 171, 175, 177, 200, 203, 204, 224, 232, 246
forgiveness 77, 154, 239
freedom 22, 27, 29, 40, 45, 61, 63-65, 79, 93, 99, 110-112, 135, 137, 139, 142, 150, 154,

156, 170, 175, 176, 196, 204, 217, 233, 234
fulfillment 31, 32, 39, 47, 80, 101, 135, 233, 238

G
gay 42, 219, 220, 222
gender 22, 94, 160, 162, 200, 210
generosity 77, 142, 199, 200
  cosmic 199, 224, 242
grief 21, 72, 92, 95, 103, 105, 106, 178
growth 25, 26, 27, 28, 29, 30, 33, 35, 39, 40, 41, 46, 47, 48, 49, 52, 53, 56, 57, 60, 61, 63, 64, 76, 79, 80, 83, 86, 87, 88, 90, 98, 101, 112, 119, 122, 124, 137, 139, 140, 148, 149, 153, 154, 155, 156, 163-165, 167-172, 174, 175, 177, 178, 183, 216, 234, 238-240

H
Hafiz 49, 241, 248
handheld mirror 57
happiness 27, 32, 39, 44, 56, 75, 80, 156, 211
Harvard Study of Adult Development 32
heroism xiv
honeymoon phase 51, 173

I
integrity 58, 162, 164, 169, 170, 173, 193, 227, 232, 245
interdependence 28, 40, 142

J
Jeffers, Susan 155
jihad 45
judgment 40, 65, 83, 89, 94, 95, 100, 121, 165, 232
Judith, Anodea 241

Jung, Carl 59

K
Kammen, Carole 65
karma 224
Kundalini 192

L
letting go 120, 154, 160, 163, 178, 186, 200, 239
LGBTQ 219, 220, 222
love
  conscious 43, 44, 88, 122, 183, 234, 246
  definition of 96
  envisioning 184
  obstacles 71, 80, 129, 130, 131
loving
  act of loving 173, 179

M
Main, Darren 68
monogamy 42, 231, 232
  high vs. low monogamy 232
morality 217, 219, 220, 223, 224, 229, 233, 245
  stages of morality 223
mortality rates 32
myths 41

N
Namaste 198, 224, 225
navigating the love frenzy 179
nonattachment 180

O
orgasm 191, 201, 210

P
passive-aggressive behavior 28
Peck, Scott 51
physical and the spiritual, the 191
power 21, 22, 33, 39, 43, 45, 55, 56, 61, 62, 63, 64, 67, 68,

94, 108, 109, 112, 116, 119, 122, 140, 143, 144, 147, 157, 159-165, 168-171, 180, 183, 184, 190, 200, 203-205, 208, 209, 211, 214, 215, 220, 221, 223, 224, 239, 241, 249
presence 22, 29, 57, 70, 112, 116, 117, 122, 198, 207, 208, 216, 234, 237, 238, 246
Princess and the Pea 155
procrastination 60
projection 56-59, 64, 238
pseudo-love 21, 43
punishment, fear of 224
purpose 21, 31, 34, 44, 46, 60, 62, 63, 65, 71, 72, 80, 86, 90, 192, 208, 209, 216, 233, 242, 249

R
Ram Dass 47, 233
Reactivity 26, 117
relationship
　challenges 39, 43, 47, 51, 55, 67, 75, 85, 91, 115
　champions 85, 86
　context for 47
　fears about relationships 130
　levels 47
　longevity 32, 174
　maintenance 75, 81, 144, 147, 156
　relationships IQ 32
religion 45, 219, 223, 224
　Religious Left 219
rescue 39, 69, 131
resistance 30, 45, 139, 140, 163, 164, 168, 169, 171, 172
Responsibility 150
retreats iii, 21, 48, 63, 73, 78, 90, 136, 137, 200, 249, 267
role models 36, 85
Romeo and Juliet 52
rules 36, 217, 224, 227, 233

S
self-awareness iv, 25, 26, 27, 31, 34, 39, 55, 56, 57, 61, 64, 96, 98, 100, 101, 106, 123, 143, 153, 160, 165, 175, 200, 208, 237, 238, 246
self-confidence 28, 118, 216
self-love 43, 44, 208
self-sabotage 60, 133, 140
self-worth 23, 39, 43, 46, 78, 131, 135, 137, 153, 176, 200, 210, 211, 215
settling 29
sexiness 207, 208
sexual energy 189, 192, 210, 211, 212, 215
sexuality
　identities 40, 189, 191
　sacred sexuality 191
　sexuality and spirituality 191-193, 197
Sexuality 42, 192, 210, 233
spiritual growth 41, 48, 52, 148, 149
spiritual traditions 192, 198, 231, 232
Sprinkle, Annie 195
suction cups 179, 180, 211, 212, 215
support system 80, 85, 175
swami cave story 49
Swimme, Brian 199

T
tantra 233
The Road Less Traveled 51
triggers 117

U
unconscious relationships 25-30, 47
Uncoupling 169
unhealthy patterns 31, 33, 92, 153

V

validation 21, 35, 39, 40, 43, 55, 68, 69, 89, 108, 135, 156, 164, 204, 208, 211-213, 234, 238
values 33, 34, 39, 43, 60, 99, 105, 131, 175, 177, 184, 219, 220
victim consciousness 65
vulnerability 29, 33, 60, 78, 94, 95, 96, 99, 119, 121, 141, 176, 201, 245

W

Wilde, Oscar 204
wounds, emotional 111

Y

yin/yang 200

CALLING ALL HEROES BOOK 2

With Heartfelt Gratitude

Thank you for reading this book. Writing it was a labor of love, rooted in the hope that it would inspire healing, deeper connection, and soulful transformation in your life and relationships. I'm honored it found its way to you.

Share the Love—Leave a Review

If *Conscious Love* resonated with you, would you take a moment to leave a review on the Amazon book page? Even just a few heartfelt words can make a big difference—they help others discover the book and remind them they're not alone on the journey. Be a voice for Conscious Love! Your words can inspire someone else's transformation.

Let Love Keep Unfolding

Stay tuned—there's more to come on the path of conscious loving. New books, retreats, and offerings are always in the works. If you'd like to continue the journey together, I invite you to join my community for exclusive resources, soulful updates, and invitations to events:

https://SoulfulPower.com
Facebook: @unleashyourinnerhero
Instagram: @christiandlh
YouTube: @soulfulpower6929

www.ingramcontent.com/pod-product-compliance
Lightning Source LLC
Chambersburg PA
CBHW072151070526
44585CB00015B/1096